*OBSERVATIONS*
*ON MODERN GARDENING*
*by*
*THOMAS WHATELY*

Garden and Landscape History

ISSN 1758-518X

General Editor
Tom Williamson

This exciting series offers a forum for the study of all aspects of the subject. It takes a deliberately inclusive approach, aiming to cover both the 'designed' landscape and the working, 'vernacular' countryside; topics embrace, but are not limited to, the history of gardens and related subjects, biographies of major designers, in-depth studies of key sites, and regional surveys.

Proposals or enquiries may be sent directly to the editor or the publisher at the addresses given below; all submissions will receive prompt and informed consideration.

Professor Tom Williamson, School of History, University of East Anglia, Norwich, Norfolk NR4 7TJ, UK.

Boydell & Brewer, PO Box 9, Woodbridge, Suffolk, England, UK IP12 3DF, UK.

Previously published

# OBSERVATIONS ON MODERN GARDENING

## BY THOMAS WHATELY

*An Eighteenth-Century Study of the*
*English Landscape Garden*

Introduction and commentary by
MICHAEL SYMES

THE BOYDELL PRESS

First published 2016
The Boydell Press, Woodbridge

ISBN 978-1-78327-102-3

The Boydell Press is an imprint of Boydell & Brewer Ltd
PO Box 9, Woodbridge, Suffolk IP12 3DF, UK
and of Boydell & Brewer Inc.
668 Mt Hope Avenue, Rochester, NY 14620-2731, USA
website: www.boydellandbrewer.com

A CIP catalogue record for this book is available from the British Library

The publisher has no responsibility for the continued existence
or accuracy of URLs for external or third-party internet websites
referred to in this book, and does not guarantee that any content
on such websites is, or will remain, accurate or appropriate

This publication is printed on acid-free paper

Printed and bound in Great Britain by
TJ International Ltd, Padstow, Cornwall

# CONTENTS

# ILLUSTRATIONS

# ACKNOWLEDGEMENTS

I am most grateful to Dr Sally Jeffery for help with the French translation of Whately's text by Latapie, Dr Patrick Eyres for advice concerning Grenville and politics, and Michael Cousins for various matters to do with the text.

All illustrations, together with the original copy of Whately's *Observations* which has been transcribed herein, are from the author's collection.

# INTRODUCTION

Thomas Whately (1726/28–1772) is generally remembered as a politician, although garden historians often see him only as the author of *Observations on Modern Gardening*. He was well known in public life and recognised also as a well-informed and cultured man with a literary bent. He was MP for Lodgershall, Wiltshire (1761–8), and for Castle Rising, Norfolk (1768–72). He served as Secretary to the Treasury in George Grenville's administration in 1764–5 and became close to Grenville, following him subsequently into opposition. Apart from politics, the two men shared a passion for landscape gardens, Grenville being the owner of Wotton, Buckinghamshire. Whately remained loyal to Grenville, defending his policies in print and, after Grenville's death, acting on behalf of his associates when Whately joined Lord North's government. He became a Commissioner on the Board of Trade in 1771, under-Secretary of State from the same year and 'Keeper of the King's private roads' in 1772, a few months before he died in only his mid-forties.

It is ironic that Grenville, steeped in an earlier generation of Whig opposition under his uncle Lord Cobham at Stowe (and one of the 'Cobham Cubs'), should have fallen foul of the new Whig opposition, the 'Rockingham Whigs', who were concerned by the increasingly pro-royal direction the government was taking. In particular, George III and Grenville adopted a hostile attitude to the American colonists, as shown most markedly in the Stamp Act, which controversially imposed a tax on them: Whately claimed it would benefit

1

them. The king himself, aware of Grenville's unpopularity, reluctantly replaced him with the second marquis of Rockingham, whose seat was at the politically charged landscape of Wentworth Woodhouse, South Yorkshire; his government, in turn, lasted only from 1765 to 1766 but repealed the Stamp Act. Whately, however, was commemorated by name in America with the naming after him of the town of Whately, Massachusetts.

Grenville was well acquainted with landscape design, both at his own property and at Stowe, which his brother Richard took over from 1749. There are apparent links with Stowe in the layout of Wotton.[1] While more of a private garden than a publicly political one, nonetheless Patrick Eyres suggests that 'Wotton was imbued with an iconography that was evocative of the interrelationship between commerce, empire and the landscape garden.'[2] Whately is commemorated by a seat at Wotton.

As a politician himself, Whately was understandably given to viewing gardens in the light of his own political beliefs, which also affected the choice of gardens in his book: he could hardly have not included Wotton. In a general sense he can be seen as complementary to Horace Walpole in championing the Whig view of the progress of gardens. In Walpole's case it was a question of seeing all developments as leading up to the climax of 'Capability' Brown: in Whately's a similar progress is implicit in his opening sentence in *Observations*: 'Gardening, in the perfection to which it has been lately brought in England...'.

Whately's ideal gardens are firmly based on Whig notions of property and freedom – freedom, that is, to create and to follow nature unconstrained by the geometry associated principally with France, where the formal garden was seen as reflecting the tyranny and absolutism of the monarchy. He can be seen to share Walpole's assertion that 'The English

Taste in Gardening is thus the growth of the English Constitution.'[3] In the book he is concerned only with large-scale landscape gardens, which were mostly the property of Whig landowners. The verse quoted on the title page shows that, for Whately, the prerequisites of a landscape garden were wealth, land ownership and taste.

Whately lived at Nonsuch Mansion, Cheam, Surrey, with his brother the Rev. Joseph Whately, who owned it from 1743. The house, built in 1730, was on the site of an old park building of the sixteenth-/seventeenth-century Nonsuch Palace, and indeed a garden wall of flint and stone harked back to Tudor times. He designed his own garden 'in very good taste', according to William Gilpin:

> particularly he changed a chalk-pit, containing about an acre, from a deformity into a beauty. He was very systematic in all his ideas – perhaps more so than the truth would bear. He planted shrubs, for instance, in such a manner, as to make a harmony among their tints, the darker or lighter to retire, or advance, as he thought the scene required.[4]

Gilpin could not, however, resist adding a caveat:

> But an attempt of this kind cannot well succeed. Foliage is such changeable colouring, that it can never be depended on. All harmony therefore from this source must be left to chance. You may happen to see in the forest a very beautiful effect of this kind: but you must look for it merely in the capriciousness of nature; & probably will not find it the next day.[5]

Whately was a close friend of Gilpin, who was headmaster at Cheam School, only half a mile from Nonsuch, from 1752 to 1777. Gilpin asked Whately to lay out his (school) garden at Cheam and declared that Whately made it very beautiful; tho Mr. G. sometimes thought (as the house was large) a square court, with the gates in front, as it was before, was more *adapted to it*; tho in *itself*, the present scene is much more beautiful.[6]

The long and close connection between Whately and Gilpin suggests that Whately absorbed some of Gilpin's 'picturesque' thinking and fostered Whately's own love of the Picturesque at a time when Gilpin was conducting his tours, though they would not be published until much later. Gilpin showed him an early draft of his tour of the eastern counties and Whately's response, in a letter of May 1769, indicates that he appreciated Gilpin's descriptive prose.[7] Nonetheless, the two did not always see eye to eye on aesthetic matters, and in any case opinions might change. In later years Gilpin, who generally disliked fictitious ruins, wrote to William Mason:

I remember beseeching Tom Whately with great earnestness, to use a heap of old stone & rubbish, of which he had the command, in something of this kind, when he laid out the garden at Nonsuch. But I had not then seen, what I since have seen, so many awkward, ridiculous, hideous attempts.[8]

Whately wrote a number of political tracts but was always drawn to literature and intended to compile a study of eight or ten characters in Shakespeare. However, the publication of *Observations* and the demands of public life precluded progress, and what was accomplished was a study of just two characters, Macbeth and Richard III, in an uncorrected state. Nevertheless Joseph Whately managed to get the work published in 1785, thirteen years after his brother's death (using the publisher of *Observations*). Whately believed that character was more worthy of discussion than other elements of Shakespeare more commonly considered and that Shakespeare's characters were 'masterly copies from nature'.[9] In selecting two such colourful figures, Whately displays a preference that accords with his taste in gardens and landscapes, the natural and the 'picturesque'.

There have been no full-length biographical or critical studies of Whately, but he features in most discussions of gardens of the time. Scholars who have focused more closely on the text include John Dixon Hunt[10] and Katja Grillner, the latter in an essay 'Experience as imagined', which compares Whately's approach with that of Joseph Heely, author of a contemporary work on Enville, Hagley and The Leasowes.[11] There have also been some exercises in historiography, but they generally concentrate on Walpole's *History of the Modern Taste in Gardening*.[12]

## EDITIONS OF THE BOOK

*Observations* was published in 1770, though some of the material may have been gathered over a number of years. It was instantly successful and in the same year a second edition appeared: it reached a third the following year. The format was modest (octavo, 5×8.5 in., 12.5×21 cm) and the book could fit into a greatcoat pocket. In 1771 it was translated into French and German and spread widely through Europe in those translations: the French edition, by Latapie, will be considered in a section of its own, while the German was by Johann Ernst Zeiber, *Betrachtungen über das heutige Gartenwesen durch Beyspiele erläutert*. The fourth English edition appeared in 1777 and the fifth in 1793, showing how much of a textbook it had become; and a sixth, illustrated, followed in 1801. Whately's name as author did not appear in any of the editions.

The first edition was published in London, as were all six, but an edition released that first year in Dublin added two extra features, an essay on design and a series of descriptions in letters. Whately's text is given in full and is then followed by the essay, which, although anonymous (like the Whately text), can be identified as George Mason's *Essay on Design in Gardening* (1768). It is to be presumed that this Dublin edition was unauthorised. The letters, addressed to the 'Rt Hon Lady J—n C—r', describe the lake, island, waterfall and old buildings of Killarney, together with a particular account of Muckross gardens there, with their rocks and views, and coverage of Killarney more generally. These letters are dated June 1760 and September 1767.

The subsequent editions, all, like the first, published by T. Payne, show some very minor changes in wording, but the 1801 publication had a distinctly new look and publisher (and was not called the sixth edition).[13] The book is much larger and the text fits into 140 pages. There were six plates to illustrate some of the gardens, plus notes by Horace Walpole and an essay. Whately had deliberately avoided using illustrations (see 'Latapie and Whately', below), but after thirty years so many prints of gardens had appeared in books that it had become an expectation. Guidebooks such as the series on Stowe had appeared with numerous vignettes, and gazetteers frequently had topographical illustrations which might well include gardens. But the main impetus was probably the publication of Repton's *Sketches and Hints on Landscape Gardening* (1795), which traded on illustration to get its messages across.

The plates, 'chiefly designed by Mr. Wollet', were only half by William Woollett – and some distance from his high-quality originals. Opposite the title page was one of Woollett's pair of engravings of Hall Barn, Buckinghamshire, in this case engraved by William Wise and published on 1 January 1798.

The remainder are distributed through the text, at positions where they relate to it. All are hand-coloured. Captions refer to owners at the time of the original print, so are forty years or so out of date. Esher Place is attributed to Woollett (actually Luke Sullivan), re-engraved by J. Walker and published in March 1798; Carlton House is not attributed to anyone (though it is in fact after Woollett) and was probably taken from a gazetteer, and is dated May 1799; Woburn Farm is ascribed to Woollett (actually Sullivan again), engraved by Walker, 1 January 1798; Painshill (Woollett/William Wise), 1 July 1798; and Hagley, attributed to Woollett (actually F. Vivares), engraved by Le Couer, 1 May 1800.

The notes by Walpole turn out to be no more than extracts filleted from his *History of the Modern Taste in Gardening* that relate to the gardens described in Whately and presented as footnotes. Following Whately's text, 'An Essay on the Different Natural Situations of Gardens' – anonymous, although subsequently attributed to S. Ward – opens with the claim that the English garden aspires to art since it combines utility with the raising of pleasing sentiments in the mind. The presumably Scottish author goes on to divide gardens into four categories: (1) highland (mountains, rocks, lakes, torrents), which produce a feeling of grandeur – equating to the Sublime; (2) romantic (valleys, woods, rivers, steep but accessible banks), producing composure of mind, perhaps even melancholy – similar to the Picturesque; (3) grounds with gentle falls and risings, a smaller scale, cultivated, much verdure (as designed by Kent and others) – productive of cheerfulness; and (4) flat – little or no sentiment except by contrast with other areas. Each branch is then considered from the practical view of the designer, with the comment that the landscapes of Poussin are the best instructor for the first.

That was the final full edition, but extracts were included in T.D. Fosbroke's edition of Gilpin's Wye Tour (1826, 34).

For a facsimile reprint of the first edition one had to wait until 1982, when Garland publishers put it out as one of several reprints of (mainly) eighteenth-century texts on gardens. This contained a brief introduction by John Dixon Hunt.

# PURPOSE, APPROACH AND COVERAGE

Whately announces at the very outset (a) that garden design has reached a state of perfection in England and (b) that it is entitled to high standing among the liberal arts. He does not offer any overt purpose for which the book is intended, nor the audience at which it is aimed (clearly both practitioners and garden visitors), but says that the business of the designer is to select from nature's scenes and materials and to combine them to best effect. He divides nature's materials into four – ground, wood, water and rocks – and adds one from art, buildings. His approach – to analyse by category – is thus made clear.

Katja Grillner has examined the approach adopted, objective and subjective, and the authoritative tone, which so impressed readers. The chapters are set out rationally, in categories that consider the subject of landscape gardening in its various aspects. These aspects are mostly material (nature's components, buildings, types of garden), but also theoretical (art, picturesque beauty and character) and illustrated by nineteen site descriptions. It is in these latter that Whately becomes subjective, giving his personal response to the various scenes, revealing not only close observation but sometimes a quite emotional reaction. In this way Whately seeks to demonstrate that gardens are to be judged aesthetically and visually but also that the emotions and the imagination can be engaged.

To Whately's categories he adds reflections on the changes wrought by the seasons or different times of day. Many examples to illustrate the categories are given, and they are by no means confined to gardens, with a number of 'natural' locations also being described.

The conclusion implies that the intention of the book was to inculcate taste and to facilitate appreciation of 'Whatever contributes to render the scenes of nature delightful', whether by 'immediate effects' or 'suggesting a train of pleasing ideas'. The garden must appeal to the senses or to the imagination (or both). Above all, the Genius of the Place – its essential spirit and character – must be respected.

## CONTEXT

Writing in 1770, Whately was able to draw on a number of landscape gardens that were by then at their zenith. Had he written twenty years later he would have been able to include some wilder, sublime gardens which were being formed, such as the great trio of Hackfall, Hafod and Hawkstone, but he was well aware of the Picturesque and responded to the Sublime in scenery if not in gardens. Although he does not refer to earlier authors by name, it is clear that he is familiar with the pronouncements on the Sublime by Edmund Burke (1757) and the steadily growing body of material linking gardens with painting and which would, in the 1790s, find fullest expression in the Picturesque Controversy involving Uvedale Price, Richard Payne Knight, Humphry Repton and others. Earlier writers who compared gardens and pictures included Alexander Pope, Arthur Young and William Shenstone, all of whom Whately could have read (and presumably had). Whately precedes the publication of Gilpin's 'picturesque' tours, but uses the term picturesque freely.

9

There were no real precedents for *Observations*. Horace Walpole's *History of the Modern Taste in Gardening* was written but would not be published for a further decade. Shenstone's 'Unconnected Thoughts on Gardening' had been published posthumously in 1764, but that was only a random collection of *pensées*. They were, however, important enough to have impressed George Mason, whose *Essay on Design in Gardening* came out four years later (and was heavily revised in 1795). Mason's approach, as was Walpole's, was to view gardens in a historical perspective, attempting to show how the English style developed (as well as demonstrating how superior it was to its formal predecessors). Whately, on the other hand, does not concern himself with garden history (except in the matter of emblem and expression, q.v.) but concentrates on explicating and assessing gardens as they existed at the time of writing.

Whately was aware of earlier detailed descriptions of gardens, however, and acknowledged Dodsley's account of The Leasowes (1764),[14] to which he refers the reader, although that does not stop him presenting a substantial description himself. He may also have known of the published accounts of Arthur Young's tours in the late 1760s through various parts of the country. He had surely read various descriptions of Stowe.

The timing of publication is significant. While we might wish the book to have come out a little later, in order to incorporate some later Georgian developments, it appeared at exactly the right time for impact on the continent. The French edition of 1771 – claimed by its translator Latapie to be the first full explication of the English garden – was just what was required by the many landowners who were embarking on pre-Revolution picturesque gardens, although Latapie prefaced his edition with a lengthy denial of English originality in the formation of the landscape garden.

# WHAT THE BOOK IS *NOT*

It is easy to misunderstand *Observations*, and in consequence to be disappointed. First and foremost, it is not a guidebook, although it was often treated as such and its small size made it eminently portable. Such descriptions as there are of gardens are usually focused on individual scenes rather than following the sequence of a visitor circuit. The random ordering of some descriptions can make it difficult to follow on the ground, and only that of The Leasowes is coherent.

Nor is it by any means comprehensive in its coverage of gardens. Whately's visiting seems to have been limited, with the result that many important sites (as they seem to us today) are omitted. For example, Whately does not appear to have gone further north than Derbyshire (where he describes Matlock and Dovedale, but no gardens), so the numerous great estates of Yorkshire are absent. And the gardens of Wales, Scotland and the south-west, from Mount Edgcumbe to Stourhead, Halswell, Hestercombe and Badminton or Cirencester Park, do not feature either, though most were well advanced by the time *Observations* came out.

It can be argued that Whately did not intend the work to be comprehensive, and that the examples given were merely to illustrate his chosen categories. As will be seen in the section on Latapie later, Whately claimed that he was well aware of other gardens, but consciously chose to limit his selection to those that would serve his purpose most effectively. But he admitted that they also constituted the gardens he knew best, presumably through visiting. We might well consider, however, in hindsight, that other examples would have supported his themes just as or more tellingly. The other consequence of a limited range of gardens is that the breadth of categories itself suffers – there might have been further categories or sub-divisions to cover such manifestations as the pictorial terrace walk or what we now often refer to as the rococo garden.

However, the book must be seen as a statement of the time as to how gardens were viewed – one man's opinion, but he was generally accepted as an authority and representative of the contemporary response to gardens. The descriptions given are often highly evocative and among the most compelling sets of evidence regarding how the gardens looked and what visitors might make of them – vital information, if we are to try to understand the sensibility of the time.

## WHATELY AND THE PICTURESQUE

Although Whately was too early for some of the wilder and more sublime garden developments, nonetheless he had a distinct taste in that direction, and 'romantic' was one of his favourite words to describe such scenes. There is only one garden, Piercefield (Persfield at the time), which fully embodies the Picturesque in his text, but the section on Rocks cites a number of 'natural' locations where the exciting side of the Picturesque comes into play. Equally, his thoughts on cascades and ruins show how much value he places on them.

The specific section, 'Of Picturesque Beauty', anticipates Repton's distinction between paintings and garden layout during the Picturesque Controversy of the 1790s by more than twenty years. The idea that there was a close connection between painting and gardening had been around at least since 1709 (Vanbrugh's plea for the retention of the medieval ruins at Blenheim), but it took Whately to show the many practical differences between the two, which Repton echoed.[15]

Whately's use of the term 'picturesque' shows that he intends it to mean 'as in a painting' rather than as the aesthetic category located between the Beautiful and Sublime as later proposed by Uvedale Price.

Whately conceded that the painting of a scene may be inspirational (and an excellent means of forming taste), and also serve as an aide-memoire afterwards, but affirmed that it lacked the dimension, space, subtlety and variety of an actual place. He concluded by reserving the term picturesque for those scenes 'in nature, as, after allowing for the differences between the arts of painting and of gardening, are fit to be formed into groupes, or to enter into a composition, where the several parts have a relation to each other'. Just as he expected the component parts of a painting to contribute to the overall composition, so he thought all elements in a garden should so combine.

## EMBLEM AND EXPRESSION

John Dixon Hunt focused on this division in an essay in *Eighteenth-Century Studies* in 1971, subsequently reprinted in the collection *Gardens and the Picturesque* (1992), and others have followed. Whately drew such a distinction in his section 'Of Character', and it is clear that he was arguing for an emotional rather than an intellectual response to gardens. It also demonstrates a preference for the naturalistic garden.

Whately decries the presence of classical statues, inscriptions and 'columns erected only to receive quotations' by saying that they are *emblematic* (pejorative to him) rather than properly expressive because they make no immediate impression and have to be thought about. Most do not relate directly to a garden anyway. He mocks the assigning of appropriate places in the garden for pagan statues, possibly in reference to Batty Langley's recommendations on the subject.[16] He is also suspicious of *imitation*, such as the creation of artificial lakes or ruins which may seem too contrived. A hermitage should be simple and rustic, not filled with accessories such as hour-glasses and beads, where the detail distracts from the idea of the building.

Whately's answer is the *expressive* garden which creates its own original character. This might be a question of concept or mood – magnificence, cheerfulness, simplicity, tranquillity. Associations and feelings aroused by, say, a ruin (if not too obviously contrived) fall into this category – they are general rather than specific. In other sections, such as that on water, Whately maintains his belief that natural elements in themselves, by virtue of their intrinsic variety, can raise different moods and reactions.

# PERCEPTION AND RESPONSE

In rejecting the 'emblematic' use of specific associations, often invoked by inscriptions, Whately makes it clear that he regards experiencing the garden as a twofold process, the immediate and the subsequent. The immediate is the visual response, which may be accompanied by an emotional reaction. Only as a secondary step does he bring in the mind, which can devise its own pictures (i.e. in imagination) prompted by the object viewed, or otherwise indulge in contemplation.

Emotional response was well established in gardens, as witness Joseph Spence's comment on Woburn Farm, Surrey, some time after 1744:

When I told Mr. Southcote that the sight of his ground near his house was always apt to lead me into a pleasing smile and into

14

a delicious sort of feeling at the heart, of which I had nothing when I was in his much nobler views along the brow of the hill, he said that Mr. Pope had often spoke of the very same effect of it on him.[17]

In 1762 Lord Kames spelled out the range of feelings that might be evoked:

Gardening, beside the emotions of beauty from regularity, order, proportion, colour, and utility, can raise emotions of grandeur, of sweetness, of gaiety, of melancholy, of wildness, and even of surprise or wonder.[18]

Following visual or emotional reactions to gardens, Whately turns to the imagination on several occasions. Addison had early in the century stated his belief in all imagination stemming from the sight of an object (in the footsteps of Locke) and that nature, which provided an infinite variety of scenes, allowed most scope and food for it.[19] Whately's idea of the imagination seems to have been first a basic and pragmatic use, as in the extent of a wood being increased by the imagination, and then in a more open, expansive form. Thus, in relation to a stretch of water, 'fancy pursues the course of the stream far beyond the view; no limits are fixed to its excursions', with an ambiguity (perhaps not intended by the author) as to whether the excursions are of the fancy or the stream. Whately is close to Addison when he declares that 'the scenes of nature have a power to affect our imagination and our sensibility', while buildings can do the same, especially ruins. In 1744 Mark Akenside had published *The Pleasures of Imagination*, a popular poem that demonstrated the continuing interest in Addison's ideas.

Whately has recourse to the word 'romantic' a number of times: it colours his description of the picturesque grounds of Piercefield, the term being closely allied both to the Picturesque and to an appeal to the imagination.

## TASTE

Like imagination, taste was central to eighteenth-century ideas of culture. It was part of an educated and civilised person's sensibility. Of course, established and recognised taste might change over the years, and those who wished to mock (such as George Mason: see below) would dismiss it as ephemeral fashion. In the case of *Observations*, Whately is manifestly trying to shape taste in laying out gardens and in appreciating them, but that is not to say that his notions are particularly original. Most stem from earlier writers such as Shenstone, and he is in tune with the times and reflects the general taste of 1770. Only in some details and in some of his categorising does he bring new thought to bear: his true originality lay in his approach.

The popularity of the book demonstrates how successful he was in spreading ideas of design and perception. It was clearly congenial to the readership both at home and abroad, and continued to influence garden philosophy for some time to come, in, for example, anticipating part of the arguments around the Picturesque in the 1790s, particularly in Repton's writings.

## ARCHIBALD ALISON

The Scottish philosopher Archibald Alison is renowned for his *Essay on the Nature and Principles of Taste* (1790), which focuses on taste and response, factors at the heart of *Observations*. It is a tribute to Whately that Alison returns repeatedly to quote from him to illustrate the categories of Beauty and Sublimity, the subjects that concern Alison most. He believes that exercise of the imagination 'increases also the Emotion of beauty or sublimity'.[20] Of the three descriptions from *Observations* quoted at length by Alison, one is to do with beauty (Hagley) and two with sublimity (Middleton Dale and the New Weir, neither of them gardens). Alison comments on Whately's rhapsodical account of the Tinian lawn at Hagley that 'It is difficult to conceive any thing more beautiful than this description, yet how much is its beauty increased by the concluding circumstance?'[21] The latter reference is to Pope's urn as glimpsed by moonlight, giving rise to contemplation.

By 'circumstance' Alison indicates specific emotional triggers, as his comment on Whately's description of the sublimity of Middleton Dale reveals: 'It is surely unnecessary to remark, how much the sublimity of this extraordinary scene is increased, by the circumstances of horror which are so firmly connected with it.'[22] Similarly, he prefaces his quotation on the New Weir with 'In the following masterly description of a very sublime scene in nature, by Mr. Whately, I doubt not but that it will be acknowledged, how much the sublimity of it is increased, by the very picturesque imagery which the occupations of the inhabitants afford.'[23] Alison believed that, when we are carried away by our reverie, the deepest emotions raised by beauty and sublimity are felt: 'Our hearts swell with feelings, which language is too weak to express',[24] and that this accords with Whately at the conclusion of his section on Character.

## WHATELY AND BROWN

Whately can be perceived to be an admirer of 'Capability' Brown in the general sense of Brown's having contributed to the declared state of perfection in which Whately found gardens at the time: but, given that his visits dated back prior to 1770, Brown was still very much active and had some of his major triumphs still to come. Furthermore, there is no praise for Brown in *Observations*, nor, indeed, is his name even mentioned (the only major designer who is named is Kent). Consequently his work is not singled out from that of his contemporaries. Whately discusses five gardens to which Brown contributed – Blenheim, Caversham, Moor Park, Wotton and Stowe – but in the case of the latter two credit has to be shared with others (Pitt and Kent respectively). Brown's lake at Blenheim is given fulsome praise, however, and is described as new, while his work at Moor Park, transforming Bridgeman's flat, even layout by means of plantings and raising hillocks, is said to have converted 'a deformity into a beauty' (the same phrase Gilpin had used in reference to Whately in his own garden). At Stowe, Brown's Grecian valley is applauded, but, as the guidebooks of the time confirm, his name was not associated with it. Whately clearly promotes the naturalistic style with which Brown is identified, but does not distinguish it from the great pictorial gardens of the mid-century that slightly pre-date Brown and which equally exhibit a naturalistic approach. Some of his comments on plantings and on water would be applicable to Brown but also to others.

Indeed, Whately seems to run counter to Brown when he launches on his section on the park, which is where one might imagine Brown would come into his own. Whately attempts to draw a distinction between garden and park where Brown endeavoured to unite them and, while admitting the two have much in common, declares 'still there are scenes in the one, which are out of reach of the other'. In particular, he is convinced that 'the spacious lawns' which are among the noblest features of a park would, in the garden, 'fatigue by their want of variety'. As is well known, Brown often brought such lawns right up to the house. The two examples of a park which Whately provides by way of illustration are Pains-hill, Surrey, and Hagley, Worcestershire, neither by Brown nor Brownian in style. Nor does he approve of the ha-ha.

Whately is also suspicious of that Brown trademark, the clump crowning a hill (as at Petworth, Sussex, or Temple Newsam, South Yorkshire). If a hill is deliberately thrown up to be so crowned it is 'artificial to a degree of disgust' and, although clumps are admissible in some circumstances, his preference is for planting carried on down the side slopes.

Another factor is Whately's promotion of the judicious de-ployment of garden buildings to create a focal point, to con-tribute to variety or to ornament a view: Brown was generally minimalist in employing architecture, with bridges rather than buildings the more common.

The omission of Brown's name, and the relative lack of attention paid to the identifiably Brownian style, meant that when the book went abroad readers would have little idea (from the text alone) of his work.

# RECEPTION AND REPUTATION

By and large *Observations* was received favourably and its author commended. Horace Walpole voiced a minor criti-cism when he adjusted his 1770 text to accommodate the newly published author and, after praising Whately as 'in-genious', queries his condemnation of *trompe l'oeil* such as 'the feigned steeple of a distant church, or an unreal bridge to disguise the termination of water'.[25] But the *Monthly Review* in 1771 summed up the general reaction by concluding (after a factual report of the contents) that the book was written with perspicuity and displayed strength, knowledge and elegance of style. Moreover, it was entertaining.[26]

Whately's reputation continued to build, and Repton, for instance, quoted him approvingly on woods in 1803, commencing his own chapter on the subject by declaring that *Observations* contains 'some remarks peculiarly applicable to the improvement of woods, and so clearly expressive of my own sentiments, that I beg to introduce the ample quotation inserted [here]'.[27] But occasionally a dissenting voice could be heard. George Mason launched a vituperative attack in his 1795 revision of *An Essay on Design in Gardening*, criticising Whately both from the standpoint of principle and on matters of taste. He reviews *Observations* as the first of a number of recent publications on gardens,[28] and comments that Whately treats garden design more like a practical art than a liberal science. Whately has no settled principles of design, nor thinks them necessary: fashion is his guide. He objects, says Mason, to successful expedients and recommends others because they have not been tried. 'The writer might have seen, that a doctrine of this sort [the following of fashion] must annihilate the utility of his own precepts after being followed, and that his book would require to be changed, as often as an almanack.'[29] Mason declares that Whately admits that very few of his precepts may not be dispensed with: 'Perhaps to have dispensed with them all might have been best.'[30]

Mason berates Whately in particular sections of *Observations* and especially when he ventures into theory, such as echoing Burke on terror: 'Writers on Gardening are strangely out of their track, when they lose themselves in the dreary wastes of metaphysical extravagancy.'[31] He finds faults from beginning to end, and objects to his categorising: 'The system is maintained with the author's usual shallowness.'[32] His conclusion is that in the end gardens did not reflect what Whately had preached: 'So little did the public think like this author, who would have converted modern gardening from a school of landscape into a field of ostentation.'[33]

The review, verging on the libellous, indicates personal animosity on the part of Mason: was he envious, perhaps, that Whately's book, coming only two years after his own first edition, had thoroughly trumped his? He was also writing twenty-five years after *Observations* first appeared, and tastes were indeed changing, with the landscape garden now being viewed with some degree of hindsight. Mason, however, was equally unhappy with contemporary 'picturesque' theory and criticised Uvedale Price in the same work.

## IMPORTANCE AND INFLUENCE

The significance of the book is that it represents the first serious attempt to analyse the landscape garden and its appeal. No previous author had tackled the subject so systematically or comprehensively (even if, today, we might regard it as far from comprehensive). It is hardly surprising, then, that it was regarded as a bible both at home and abroad, and influenced taste and the way of experiencing gardens. The tone is authoritative and would lead readers to assume that Whately knew what he was talking about.

The book solidified the concept of the English landscape garden, although that term did not come into being until the 1940s: as is evident from its title, Whately champions it as Modern Gardening, thus stressing its up-to-dateness as well as implying its superiority to what had gone before. To emphasise modernity represents a sea change from the Augustan age early in the century, when so much culture was based on precedent and the authority of the ancients. This can be seen in the context of an Enlightenment confident in a progress that, for example, produced the Industrial Revolution at more or less the same time.

While the number of gardens described may be limited, and usually incomplete or not logically ordered, those descriptions he provided are often the fullest that we have and the most important for visualising how the gardens looked at the time and what was most significant in them.

Its influence at home can be seen not only in the number of editions it went through in thirty years but in the fact that it coloured so many subsequent discussions and writings, whether Whately was specifically acknowledged or not. No one thereafter could write in ignorance of *Observations* – not, anyway, until the nineteenth century. The major authors of the day – William Marshall, Repton and, later, Loudon – all paid heed to it. It was regarded as the standard text on the subject.

Abroad it provided an incentive for authors to enter the same territory. C.-H. Watelet's *Essai sur les jardins* (1774) was followed by Jean-Marie Morel's *Théorie des jardins* (1776) and the Marquis de Girardin's *De la composition des paysages* (1777), each taking Whately on board in his own way, adopting his approach or embodying some of his thinking. Hirschfeld, correspondingly, drew on Whately in his massive *Theorie der Gartenkunst* (1779–85), the most important of German texts. These authors did not always agree with Whately, but they took him seriously and acknowledged his standing. We have seen that the French and, to a lesser extent, the German translations of Whately spread widely across Europe, including Russia, bringing him to a very wide audience.

*Observations* crossed the Atlantic as well. It was not only home tourists who took it around with them as a quasi-guidebook: Thomas Jefferson, on his itinerary of English gardens in 1786, remarked on The Leasowes as 'only a grazing farm with a path round it',[34] the wording betraying his debt to Whately (the *Observations* accompanied him on his tours). Jefferson took up some elements of The Leasowes when designing Monticello back home, probably as a result of his visit combined with something from Whately. And, although it was the French edition which permeated Europe, Whately in English was taken around gardens by F.M. Piper during the 1770s and annotated: when he returned home to Sweden, his was the main influence in promulgating ideas of the landscape garden there. Likewise, the French architect F.-J. Bélanger was instrumental in spreading ideas about the landscape garden in France after visiting England for the second time in 1777 and clearly following Whately in his choice of places to visit and sketch – among others, Stowe, Painshill, Enfield Chase, Ilam, The Leasowes and Claremont, plus two of the Peak District sights, Dovedale and Matlock.

For present-day readers the book has both historical and practical importance. The theoretical aspects are of more academic interest, but the descriptions are not only evocative to read but can often help in the conservation and restoration of historic gardens, as well as in promoting an understanding of the landscape garden and how one might respond to it.

# NOTE ON THE TEXT

The following transcription of the third edition (August 1771) of Whately's book preserves the original spelling and punctuation, except in a small number of cases which are clearly typographical errors (and which were corrected in later editions). However, Whately (or his printer) was inconsistent in spelling some words and these have been left as printed, so both forms will be found (agreable/agreeable; characterize/characterise; disagreable/disagreeable; independant/independent; antient/ancient; strait/straight; inclosure/enclosure; shrubery/shrubbery; tranquility/tranquillity; connexion/connection; heighth/height; stile/style; vallies/valleys; greenswerd/green-swerd – also found as two separate words, green swerd).

Figure 1. Title page of *Observations on Modern Gardening*, 3rd edn, 1771.

# OBSERVATIONS

## ON

# MODERN GARDENING

### ILLUSTRATED BY

## DESCRIPTIONS

Where Wealth, enthron'd in Nature's pride,
With Taste and Bounty by her side,
  And holding Plenty's horn,
Sends Labour to pursue the toil,
Art to improve the happy soil,
  And Beauty to adorn.      E.

## THE THIRD EDITION.

## LONDON,

Printed for T. PAYNE, at the Mews-gate.

MDCCLXXI.

# TABLE OF THE CONTENTS.

OF WATER.

OF ROCKS.

OF BUILDINGS.

OF ART.

OF PICTURESQUE BEAUTY.

OF CHARACTER.

OF THE GENERAL SUBJECT.

OF A FARM.

# INTRODUCTION.

## I.

GARDENING, in the perfection to which it has been lately brought in England, is entitled to a place of considerable rank among the liberal arts. It is as superior to landskip painting, as a reality to a representation: it is an exertion of fancy; a subject for taste; and being released now from the restraints of regularity, and enlarged beyond the purposes of domestic convenience, the most beautiful, the most simple, the most noble scenes of nature are all within its province: for it is no longer confined to the spots from which it borrows its name, but regulates also the disposition and embellishments of a park, a farm, or a riding; and the business of a gardener is to select and to apply whatever is great, elegant, or characteristic in any of them; to discover and to shew all the advantages of the place upon which he is employed; to supply its defects, to correct its faults, and to improve its beauties. For all these operations, the objects of nature are still his only materials. His first enquiry, therefore, must be into the means by which those effects are attained in nature, which he is to produce; and into those properties in the objects of nature, which should determine him in the choice and arrangement of them.

Nature, always simple, employs but four materials in the composition of her scenes, *ground, wood, water*, and *rocks*. The cultivation of nature has introduced a fifth species, the *buildings* requisite for the accommodation of men. Each of these again admits of varieties in figure, dimensions, colour, and situation. Every landskip is composed of these parts only; every beauty in a landskip depends on the application of their several varieties.

## Of GROUND.

## II.

The shape of ground must be either a *convex*, a *concave*, or a *plane*; in terms less technical called a *swell*, a *hollow*, and a *level*. By combinations of these are formed all the irregularities of which ground is capable; and the beauty of it depends on the degrees and the proportions in which they are blended.

Both the convex and the concave are forms in themselves of more variety, and may therefore be admitted to a greater extent than a plane; but levels are not totally inadmissible. The preference unjustly shewn to them in the old gardens, where they prevailed almost in exclusion of every other form, has raised a prejudice against them. It is frequently reckoned an excellence in a piece of made ground, that every the least part of it is uneven; but then it wants one of the three great varieties of ground, which may sometimes be intermixed with the other two. A gentle concave declivity falls and spreads easily on a flat; the channels between several swells degenerate into mere gutters, if some breadth be not given to the bottoms by flattening them; and in many other instances, small portions of an inclined or horizontal plane may be introduced into an irregular composition. Care only must be taken to keep them down as subordinate parts, and not to suffer them to become principal.

There are, however, occasions on which a plane may be principal: a hanging level often produces effects not otherwise attainable. A large dead flat, indeed, raises no other idea than of satiety: the eye finds no amusement, no repose on such a level: it is fatigued, unless timely relieved by an adequate termination; and the strength of that termination will compensate for its distance. A very wide plain, at the foot of a mountain, is less tedious than one of much less compass, surrounded only by hillocks. A flat therefore of considerable extent may be hazarded in a garden, provided the boundaries also be considerable in proportion; and if, in addition to their importance, they become still more interesting by their beauty, then the facility and distinctness with which they are seen over a flat, make the whole an agreable composition. The greatness and the beauty of the boundary are not, however, alone sufficient; the form of it is of still more consequence. A continued range of the noblest wood, or the finest hill, would not cure the insipidity of a flat: a less important, a less pleasing boundary, would be more effectual, if it traced a more varied outline; if it advanced sometimes boldly forward, sometimes retired into deep recesses; broke all the sides into parts, and marked even the plain itself with irregularity.

At Moor Park*, on the back front of the house, is a lawn of about thirty acres, absolutely flat; with falls below it on one hand, and heights above it on the other. The rising ground is divided into three great parts, each so distinct and so different, as to have the effect of several hills. That nearest to the house shelves gently under an open grove of noble trees, which hang on the declivity, and advance beyond it on the plain. The next is a large hill, pressing forward, and covered with wood from the top to the bottom. The third is a bold steep, with a thicket falling down the steepest part, which makes it appear still more precipitate: but the rest of the slope is bare; only the brow is crowned with wood, and towards the bottom is a little groupe of trees. These heights, thus finely characterised in themselves, are further distinguished by their appendages. The small, compact groupe near the foot, but still on the descent, of the further hill, is contrasted by a large straggling clump, some way out upon the lawn, before the middle eminence. Between this and the first hill, under two or three trees which cross the opening, is seen to great advantage a winding glade, which rises beyond them, and marks the separation. This deep

---

\* The seat of Sir Lawrence Dundass, near Rickmansworth in Hertfordshire.

recess, the different distances to which the hills advance, the contrast in their forms, and their accompaniments, cast the plain on this side into a most beautiful figure. The other side and the end were originally the flat edge of a descent, a harsh, offensive termination; but it is now broken by several hillocks, not diminutive in size, and considerable by the fine clumps which distinguish them. They recede one beyond another, and the outline waves agreably amongst them. They do more than conceal the sharpness of the edge; they convert a deformity into a beauty, and greatly contribute to the embellishment of this most lovely scene; a scene, however, in which the flat is principal; and yet a more varied, a more beautiful landskip, can hardly be desired in a garden.

## III.

A plain is not, however, in itself interesting; and the least deviation from the uniformity of its surface changes its nature; as long as the flat remains, it depends on the objects around for all its variety, and all its beauty; but convex and concave forms are generally pleasing; and the number of degrees and combinations into which they may be cast is infinite: those forms only in each which are perfectly regular must be avoided; a semicircle can never be tolerable: small portions of large circles blended together: or lines gently curved, which are not parts of any circle; a hollow sinking but little below a level; a swell very much flatten'd at the top; are commonly the most agreable figures.

In ground which lies beautifully, the concave will generally prevail; within the same compass it shews more surface than a swell; all the sides of the latter are not visible at the same time, except in a few particular situations; but it is only in a few particular situations, that any part of a hollow is concealed; earth seems to have been accumulated to raise the one, and taken away to sink the other. The concave, therefore, appears the lighter, and for the most part it is the more elegant shape; even the slopes of a swell can hardly be brought down, unless broken now and then into hollows, to take off from the heaviness of the mass. There are, however, situations where the convex form should be preferred: a hollow just below the brow of a hill reduces it to a narrow ridge, which has a poor meagre appearance; and an abrupt fall will never seem to join with a concave form immediately above it; a sharp edge divides them; and to connect them, that edge must be rounded, or at least flattened; which is, in fact, to interpose a convex or a level.

## IV.

In made ground, the connection is, perhaps, the principal consideration. A swell which wants it is but a heap; a hollow but a hole; and both appear artificial: the one seems placed upon a surface to which it does not belong; the other dug into it. On the great scale of nature, indeed, either may be so considerable in itself, as to make its relation to any other almost a matter of indifference; but on the smaller scale of a garden, if the parts are disjointed, the effect of the whole is lost; and the union of all is not more than sufficient to preserve an idea of greatness and importance, to spots which must be varied, and cannot be spacious. Little inequalities are besides in nature usually well blended together; all lines of separation have, in a course of time, been filled up; and therefore, when in made ground they are left open, that ground appears artificial.

Even where artifice is avowed, a breach in the connection offends the eye. The use of a fosse is merely to provide a fence, without obstructing the view. To blend the garden with the country is no part of the idea: the cattle, the objects, the culture, without the sunk fence, are discordant to all within, and keep up the division. A fosse may open the most polished lawn to a corn-field, a road, or a common, though they mark the very point of separation. It may be made on purpose to shew objects which cannot, or ought not to be in the garden; as a church, or a mill, a neighbouring gentleman's seat, a town, or a village; and yet no consciousness of the existence can reconcile us to the sight of this division. The most obvious disguise is to keep the hither above the further bank all the way; so that the latter may not be seen at a competent distance: but this alone is not always sufficient; for a division appears, if an uniformly continued line, however faint, be discernible; that line, therefore, must be broken; low but ex-tended hillocks may sometimes interrupt it; or the shape on one side may be continued, across the sunk fence, on the other; as when the ground sinks in the field, by beginning the declivity in the garden. Trees too without, connected with those within, and seeming part of a clump or a grove there, will frequently oblit-erate every trace of an interruption. By such, or other means, the line may be, and should be hid or disguised; not for the purpose of deception, (when all is done, we are seldom deceived) but to preserve the continued surface entire.

If, where no union is intended, a line of separation is disa-greeable, it must be disgusting, when it breaks the connection between the several parts of the same piece of ground. That con-nection depends on *the junction of each part to those about it*, and on *the relation of every part to the whole*. To complete the former, such shapes should be contiguous as most readily unite; and the actual division between them should be anxiously concealed. If a swell descends upon a level; if a hollow sinks from it, the level is an abrupt termination, and a little rim marks it distinctly. To cover that rim, a short sweep at the foot of the swell, a small rotundity at the entrance of the hollow, must be interposed. In every instance, when ground changes its direction, there is a point where the change is effected, and that point should never appear; some other shapes, uniting easily with both extremes, must be thrown in to conceal it. But there must be no uniformity even in these connections; if the same sweep be carried all round the bottom of a swell, the fame rotundity all round the top of a hollow, though the junction be perfect, yet the art by which it is made is apparent, and art must never appear. The manner of concealing the separation should itself be disguised; and different degrees of cavity and rotundity; different shapes and dimensions to the little parts thus distinguished by degrees; and those parts, breaking in one place more, in another less, into the principal forms which are to be united; produce that variety with which all nature abounds, and without which ground cannot be natural.

V.

The relation of all the parts to the whole, when clearly marked, facilitates their junction with each other: for the common bond of union is then perceived, before there has been time to examine the subordinate connections; and if these should be deficient in some niceties, the defect is lost in the general impression. But any part which is at variance with the rest, is not barely a blemish in itself: it spreads disorder as far as its influence extends; and the confusion is in proportion as the other parts are more or less adapted, to point out any *particular direction*, or to mark any *peculiar character* in the ground.

If in ground all descending one way, a piece is twisted another, the general fall is obstructed by it; but if all the parts incline in the same direction, it is hardly credible how small a declivity will seem to be considerable. An appearance even of steepness may be given to a very gentle descent, by raising hillocks upon it, which shall lean to the point, whither all the rest are tending; for the eye measures from the top of the highest, to the bottom of the lowest ground; and when the relation of the parts is well preserved, such an effect from one is transfused over the whole.

But they should not, therefore, all lie exactly in the same direction: some may seem to point to it directly, others to incline very much, others but little, some partially, some entirely. If the direction be strongly marked on a few principal parts, great liberties may be taken with the others, provided none of them are turned the contrary way. The general idea must, however, be preserved, clear even of a doubt. A hillock which only intercepts the sight, if it does not contribute to the principal effect, is at the best an unnecessary excrescence; and even an interruption in the general tendency, though it hide nothing, is a blemish. On a descent, any hollow, any fall, which has not an outlet to lower ground, is a hole: the eye skips over it instead of being continued along it; it is a gap in the composition.

There may indeed be occasions, when we should rather wish to check, than to promote, the general tendency. Ground may proceed too hastily towards its point; and we have equal power to retard, or to accelerate, the fall. We can slacken the precipitancy of a steep, by breaking it into parts, some of which shall incline less, than the whole before inclined, to the principal direction; and by turning them quite away, we may even change the course of the descent. These powers are of use in the larger scenes, where the several great parts often lie in several directions; and if they are thereby too strongly contrasted, or led towards points too widely asunder, every art should be exerted to bring them nearer together, to assimilate, and to connect them. As scenes encrease in extent they become more impatient of controul: they are not only less manageable, but ought to be less restrained; they require more variety and contrast. But still the same principles are applicable to the least, and to the greatest, tho' not with equal severity: neither ought to be rent to pieces; and though a small neglect, which would distract the one, may not disturb the other, yet a total disregard of all the principles of union, is alike productive of confusion in both.

## VI.

The *style* also of every part, must be accommodated to the character of the whole; for every piece of ground is distinguished by certain properties: it is either tame or bold; gentle or rude; continued or broken; and if any variety, inconsistent with those properties, be obtruded, it has no other effect than to weaken one idea without raising another. The insipidity of a flat is not taken away by a few scattered hillocks; a continuation of uneven ground can alone give the idea of inequality. A large, deep, abrupt break, among easy swells and falls, seems at the best but a piece left unfinished, and which ought to have been softened: it is not more natural, because it is more rude; nature forms both the one and the other, but seldom mixes them together. On the other hand, a small fine polished form, in the midst of rough, mishapen ground, though more elegant than all about it, is generally no better than a patch, itself disgraced, and disfiguring the scene. A thousand instances might be adduced to shew, that the prevailing idea ought to pervade every part, so far at least indispensably as to exclude whatever distracts it; and as much further as possible to accommodate the character of the ground to that of the scene it belongs to.

On the same principle, the *proportion* of the parts may often be adjusted; for though their size must be very much governed by the extent of the place; and a feature which would fill up a small spot, may be lost in a large one: though there are forms of a particular cast, which appear to advantage only within certain dimensions, and ought not therefore to be applied, where they have not room enough, or where they must occupy more space than becomes them; yet independant of these considerations, a character of greatness belongs to some scenes, which is not measured by their extent, but raised by other properties, sometimes only by the proportional largeness of their parts. On the contrary, where elegance characterises the spot, the parts should

not only be small, but diversified besides with subordinate inequalities, and little delicate touches every where scattered about
them. Striking effects, forcible impressions, whatever seems to
require effort, disturbs the enjoyment of a scene intended to
amuse and to please.

In other instances, similar considerations will determine
rather the *number* than the proportion of the parts. A place may
be distinguished by its simplicity, which many divisions would
destroy; another spot, without any pretensions to elegance, may
be remarkable for an appearance of richness: a multiplicity of
objects will give that appearance, and a number of parts in the
ground will contribute to the profusion. A scene of gaiety is improved by the same means; the objects and the parts may differ
in style, but they must be numerous in both. Sameness is dull;
the purest simplicity can at the most render a place composed
of large parts placid; the sublimest ideas only make it striking; it
is always grave; to enliven it, numbers are wanting.


## VII.

But ground is seldom beautiful or natural without *variety*, or
even without contrast; and the precautions which have been
given, extend no further than to prevent variety from degenerat-
ing into inconsistency, and contrast into contradiction. Within
the extremes, nature supplies an inexhaustible fund; and variety
thus limited, so far from destroying, improves the general effect.
Each distinguished part makes a separate impression; and all
bearing the same stamp, all concurring to the same end, every
one is an additional support to the prevailing idea: that is multiplied; it is extended; it appears in different shapes; it is shewn
in several lights; and the variety illustrates the relation.

But variety wants not this recommendation; it is always desireable where it can be properly introduced; and an accurate ob-

server will see in every *form* several circumstances by which it is distinguished from every other. If the scene be mild and quiet, he will place together those which do not differ widely; and he will gradually depart from the similitude. In ruder scenes, the succession will be less regular, and the transitions more sudden. The character of the place must determine the degree of difference between forms which are contiguous. Besides distinctions in the shapes of ground, differences in their *situations* and their *dimensions* are sources of variety. The position will alter the effect, tho' the figure be the same; and for particular effects, a change only in the distance may be striking. If that be considerable, a succession of similar shapes sometimes occasions a fine perspective; but the diminution will be less marked, that is, the effect will be less sensible, if the forms are not nearly alike: we take more notice of one difference, when there is no other. Sometimes a very disagreeable effect, produced by too close a resemblance of shapes, may be remedied only by an alteration in the size. If a steep descends in a succession of abrupt falls, nearly equal, they have the appearance of steps, and are neither pleasing nor wild; but if they are made to differ in height and length, the objection is removed: and at all times a difference in the dimensions will be found to have a greater effect, than in speculation we should be inclined to ascribe to it, and will often disguise a similarity of figure.

## VIII.

It also contributes, perhaps more than any other circumstance, to the perfection of those *lines*, which the eye traces along the parts of a piece of ground, when it glances over several together. No variety of form compensates for the want of it. An undulating line composed of parts all elegant in themselves, all judiciously contrasted and happily united, but equal one to another, is far from the line of beauty. A long strait line has no variety at all;

and a little deviation into a curve, if there be still a continued uniformity, is but a trifling amendment. Though ground all falling the same way requires every attention to its general tendency, yet the eye must not dart down the whole length immediately in one direction, but should be insensibly conducted towards the principal point with some circuity and delay. The channels between hillocks ought never to run in straight, nor even regularly curved lines; but winding gently among them, and constantly varying in form and in dimensions, should gradually find their way. The beauty of a large hill, especially when seen from below, is frequently impaired by the even continuation of its brow. An attempt to break it by little knoles is seldom successful; they seem separate independent hillocks artificially put on. The intended effect may indeed be produced by a large knole descending in some places lower than in others, and rooted at several points into the hill. The same end may be attained by carrying some channel or hollow on the side upwards, till it cut the continued line; or by bringing the brow forward in one place, and throwing it back in another; or by forming a secondary ridge a little way down the side, and casting the ground above it into a different, though not opposite direction to the general descent. Any of these expedients will at least draw the attention off from the defect; but if the break were to divide the line into equal parts, another uniformity would be added, without removing the former; for regularity always suggests a suspicion of artifice; and artifice detected, no longer deceives. Our imaginations would industriously join the broken parts, and the idea of the continued line would be restored.

## IX.

Whatever break be chosen, the position of it must be oblique to the line which is to be broken. A rectangular division produces sameness; there is no *contrast* between the forms it divides; but if it be oblique, while it diminishes the part on one side, it enlarges that on the other. Parallel lines are liable to the same objection as those at right angles: though each by itself be the perfect line of beauty, yet if they correspond, they form a shape between them, whose sides want contrast. On the same principle, forms will sometimes be introduced, less for their intrinsic than their occasional merit, in contrasting happily with those about them: each sets off the other; and together they are a more agreeable composition than if they had been more beautiful, but at the same time more similar.

One reason why tame scenes are seldom interesting is, that though they often admit of many varieties, they allow of few, and those only faint contrasts. We may be pleased by the number of the former, but we can be struck only by the force of the latter. These ought to abound in the larger and bolder scenes of a garden, especially in such as are formed by an assemblage of many distinct and considerable parts thrown together; as when several rising grounds appear one beyond another, a fine swell seen above a slanting sweep which runs before it, has a beautiful effect, which a nearer resemblance would destroy: and (except in particular instances) a close similarity between lines which either cross, or face, or rise behind one another, makes a poor uniform, disagreeable composition.

X.

The application of any of the foregoing observations to the still greater scenes of nature, would carry me at present too far; nor could it well be made, before the other constituent parts of those scenes, wood, water, rocks, and buildings, have been taken into consideration. The rules which have been given, if such hints deserve the name of rules, are chiefly applicable to ground which may be managed by a spade; and even there they are only general, not universal: few of them are without exception; very few which, on particular occasions, may not be dispensed with. Many of the above remarks are, however, so far of use in scenes the furthest from our reach, as they may assist in direct-ing our choice of those parts which are in our power to shew, or to conceal, though not to alter. But in converting them to this purpose, a caution, which has more than once been alluded to, must always be had in remembrance; never to suffer general considerations to interfere with *extraordinary great effects*, which rise superior to all regulations, and perhaps owe part of their force to their deviation from them. Singularity causes at least surprise, and surprise is allied to astonishment. These effects are not, however, attached merely to objects of enormous size; they frequently are produced by a greatness of style and character, within such an extent as ordinary labour may modify, and the compass of a garden include. The caution therefore may not be useless within these narrow bounds; but nature proceeds still further, beyond the utmost verge to which art can follow; and in scenes licentiously wild, not content with contrast, forces even contradictions to unite. The grotesque discordant shapes which are often there confusedly tumbled together, might sufficiently justify the remark. But the caprice does not stop here; to mix with such shapes a form perfectly regular, is still more extrava-gant; and yet the effect is sometimes so wonderful, that we can-not wish the extravagance corrected. It is not unusual to see a conical hill standing out from a long, irregular, mountainous ridge, and greatly improving the view: but at Ilam* such a hill is thrown into the midst of the rudest scene, and almost fills up an abyss, sunk among huge, bare, mishapen hills, whose unwieldy parts, and uncouth forms, cut by the tapering lines of the cone, appear more savage from the opposition; and the effect would evidently be stronger, were the figure more complete: for it

* The seat of Mr. Porte, near Ashbourne in Derbyshire.

does not rise quite to a point, and the want of perfect regularity seems a blemish. Whether such a mixture of contrarieties would for a length of time be engaging, can be known only to those who are habituated to the spot. It certainly at first sight rivets the attention. But the conical hill is the most striking object; in such a situation it appears more strange, more fantastic, than the rude shapes which are heaped about it; and together they suit the character of the place, where nature seems to have delighted to bring distances together; where two rivers, which are ingulphed many miles asunder, issue from their subterraneous passages, the one often muddy when the other is clear, within a few paces of each other; but they appear only to lose themselves again, for they immediately unite their streams, just in time to fall together into another current, which also runs through the garden. Such whimsical wonders, however, lose their effect, when represented in a picture, or mimicked in ground artificially laid. They there want that vastness which constitutes their force; that reality which ascertains the caprice. As accidents they may surprise; but they are not objects of choice.

## XI.

To determine the choice to its proper objects is the purpose of the foregoing observations. Some of the principles upon which they are founded will be applicable also, and perhaps without further explanation, to the other constituent parts of the scenes of nature: they will there be often more obvious than in ground. But this is not a place for the comparison; the subject now is ground only. It is not, however, foreign to that subject to observe, that the effects which have been recommended, may sometimes be produced by wood alone, without any alteration in the ground itself: a tedious continued line may by such means be broken; it is usual for this purpose to place several little clumps along a brow; but if they are small and numerous, the artifice is weak and apparent: an equal number of trees collected into one or two large masses, and dividing the line into very unequal parts, is less suspicious, and obliterates the idea of sameness with more certainty. Where several similar lines are seen together, if one be planted, and the other bare, they become contrasts to each other. A hollow in certain situations, has been mentioned as a disagreeable interruption in a continued surface; but filled with wood, the heads of the trees supply the vacancy; the irregularity is preserved; even the inequalities of the depth are in some measure shewn; and a continuation of surface is provided. Rising ground may on the other hand, be in appearance raised still higher, by covering it with wood, of humble growth towards the bottom, and gradually taller as it ascends. An additional mark of the inclination of falling ground may also be obtained, by placing a few trees in the same direction, which will strongly point out the way; whereas plantations athwart a descent, bolster up the ground, and check the fall; but obliquely crossing it they will often divert the general tendency; the ground will in some measure assume their direction, and they will make a variety, not a contradiction. Hedges, or continued plantations, carried over uneven ground, render the irregularity more conspicuous, and frequently mark little inequalities, which would otherwise escape observation: or if a line of trees run close upon the edge of an abrupt fall, they give it depth and importance. By such means a view may be improved; by similar means, in more confined spots, very material purposes may be answered.

## Of WOOD.

### XII.

In these instances the ground is the principal consideration: but previous to any enquiry into the greater effects of wood, when it is itself an object, an examination of the *characteristic differences* of trees and shrubs is necessary. I do not mean botanical distinctions; I mean apparent, not essential varieties; and these must be obvious and considerable, to merit regard in the disposition of the objects they distinguish.

Trees and shrubs are of different *shapes*, *greens*, and *growths*.

The varieties in their shapes may be reduced to the following heads.

Some thick with branches and foliage have almost *an appearance of solidity*, as the beech and the elm, the lilac and seringa. Others thin of boughs and of leaves seem *light and airy*, as the ash and the arbele, the common arbor vitae and the tamarisk.

There is a *mean betwixt the two extremes*, very distinguishable from both, as in the bladder-nut, and the ashen-leaved maple.

They may again be divided into those whose *branches begin from the ground*, and those which *shoot up in a stem before their branches begin*\*. Trees which have some, not much clear stem, as several of the firs, belong to the former class; but a very short stem will rank a shrub, such as the althaea, in the latter.

Of those whose branches begin from the ground, some rise in a *conical figure*, as the larch, the cedar of Lebanon, and the holly; some *swell out in the middle of their growth, and diminish at both ends*, as the Weymouth pine, the mountain ash, and the lilac; and some are *irregular and bushy* from the top to the bottom, as the evergreen oak, the Virginian cedar, and Guelder rose.

There is a great difference between one whose *base is very large*, and another *whose base is very small*, in proportion to its height: the cedar of Lebanon, and the cypress, are instances of this difference; yet in both the branches begin from the ground.

---

\* Perhaps there are few, if any, which do not put forth branches from the bottom; but in some, the lower branches are, from various circumstances, generally destroyed; and they appear, at a certain period of their growth, to have shot up into a stem before their branches began.

The heads of those which shoot up into a stem before their branches begin, sometimes are *slender cones*, as of many firs: sometimes are *broad cones*, as of the horse-chesnut; sometimes they are *round*, as of the stone pine, and most sorts of fruit trees; and sometimes *irregular*, as of the elm. Of this last kind there are many considerable varieties.

The branches of some grow *horizontally*, as of the oak. In others they *tend upwards*, as in the almond, and in several sorts of broom, and of willows. In others they *fall*, as in the lime, and the acacia; and in some of these last they *incline obliquely*, as in many of the firs; in some they *hang directly down*, as in the weeping willow.

These are the most obvious great distinctions in the shapes of trees and shrubs. The differences between shades of green cannot be so considerable; but these also will be found well deserving of attention.

Some are of a *dark green*, as the horse-chesnut, and the yew; some of a *light green*, as the lime, and the laurel; some of a *green tinged with brown*, as the Virginian cedar; some of a *green tinged with white*, as the arbele, and the sage tree; and some of a *green tinged with yellow*, as the ashen-leaved maple, and the Chinese arbor vitae. The variegated plants also are generally entitled to be classed with the white, or the yellow, by the strong tincture of the one or the other of those colours on their leaves.

Other considerations concerning colours will soon be suggested; the present enquiry is only into great fixed distinctions: those in the shapes and the greens of trees and shrubs have been mentioned; there are others as great and as important in their growths; but they are too obvious to deserve mentioning. Every gradation, from the most humble to the most lofty, has, in certain situations, particular effects: it is unnecessary to divide them into stages.

## XIII.

One principal use in settling these characteristic distinctions, is to point out the stores whence varieties may at all times be readily drawn, and the causes by which sometimes inconsistencies may be accounted for. Trees which differ but in one of these circumstances, whether of shape, or green, or of growth, though they agree in every other, are sufficiently distinguished for the purpose of variety: if they differ in two or three, they become contrasts; if in all, they are opposites, and seldom groupe well together. But there are intermediate degrees, by which the most distant may be reconciled: the upright branches of the almond mix very ill with the falling boughs of the weeping willow; but an interval filled with other trees, in figure between the two extremes, renders them at least not unsightly in the same plantation. Those, on the contrary, which are of one character, and are distinguished only as the characteristic mark is strongly or faintly impressed upon them, as a young beech and a birch, an acacia and a larch, all pendant, tho' in different degrees, form a beautiful mass, in which unity is preserved without sameness; and still finer groupes may often be produced by greater deviations from uniformity into contrast.

Occasions to shew the effects of particular shapes in certain situations will hereafter so frequently occur, that a further illustration of them now would be needless. But there are besides, sometimes in trees, and commonly in shrubs, still *more minute varieties*, in the turn of the branches, in the form and the size of the foliage, which generally catch, and often deserve attention. Even the texture of the leaves frequently occasions many different appearances; some have a stiffness, some an agility, by which they are more or less proper for several purposes: on many is a gloss, very useful at times to enliven, at other times too glittering for the hue of the plantation. But all these inferior varieties are below our notice in the consideration of great effects: they are of consequence only where the plantation is near to the sight; where it skirts a home scene, or borders the side of a walk: and in a shrubbery, which in its nature is little, both in style and in extent, they should be anxiously sought for. The noblest wood is not indeed disfigured by them; and when a wood, having served as a great object to one spot, becomes in another the edge of a walk, little circumstances, varying with ceaseless change along the outline, will then be attended to; but wherever these minute varieties are fitting, the grossest taste will feel the propriety, and the most cursory observation, will suggest the distinctions; a detail of all would be endless; nor can they be reduced into classes. To range the shrubs and small trees so that they may mutually set off the beauties, and conceal the blemishes of each other; to aim at no effects which depend on a nicety for their success, and which the soil, the exposure, or the season of the day may destroy; to attend more to the groupes than to the individuals; and consider the whole as a plantation, not as a collection of plants, are the best general rules which can be given concerning them.

## XIV.

The different tints of greens may seem at first sight to be rather minute varieties than characteristic distinctions; but upon experience it will be found, that from small beginnings they lead to material consequences; that they are more important on the broad expanse, than along the narrow outline of a wood; and that by their union, or their contrast, they produce effects not to be disregarded in scenes of extent and of grandeur.

A hanging wood in autumn is enriched with colours, whose beauty cheers the approaches of the inclement season they forebode: but when the trees first droop, while the verdure as yet only begins to fade, they are no more than stronger tints of those colours with which the greens in their vigour are shaded; and which now are succeeded by a paler white, a brighter yellow, or a darker brown. The effects are not different; they are only more faintly impressed at one time than another; but when they are strongest they are most observable. The fall of the leaf, therefore, is the time to learn the species, the order, and the proportion of tints, which blended, will form *beautiful masses*; and, on the other hand, to distinguish those which are *incompatible* near together.

The peculiar beauty of the tints of red cannot then escape observation, and the want of them through the summer months must be regretted; but that want, though it cannot perfectly, may partially, be supplied; for plants have a *permanent* and an *accidental* colour. The permanent is always some shade of green; but any other may be the accidental colour; and there is none which so many circumstances concur to produce as a red. It is assumed in succession by the bud, the blossom, the berry, the bark, and the leaf. Sometimes it profusely overspreads; at other times it dimly tinges the plant; and a *reddish green* is generally the hue of those plants, on which it lasts long, or frequently returns.

Admitting this, at least for many months in the year, among the characteristic distinctions, a large piece of red green, with a narrow edging of dark green along the further side of it, and beyond that a piece of light green larger than the first, will be found to compose a beautiful mass. Another, not less beautiful, is a yellow green nearest to the eye, beyond that a light green, then a brown green, and lastly a dark green. The dark green must be the largest, the light green the next in extent, and the yellow green the least of all.

From these combinations, the agreements between particular tints may be known. A light green may be next either to a yellow or a brown green, and a brown to a dark green; all in considerable quantities; and a little rim of dark green may border on a red or a light green. Further observations will shew, that the yellow and the white greens connect easily; but that a large quantity of the light, the yellow, or the white greens, does not mix well with a large quantity also of the dark green; and that to form a pleasing mass, either the dark green must be reduced to a mere edging, or a brown, or an intermediate green, must be interposed: that the red, the brown, and the intermediate greens, agree among themselves; and that any of them may be joined to any other tint; but that the red green will bear a larger quantity of the light than of the dark green near it; nor does it seem so proper a mixture with the white green as with the rest.

In massing these tints, an attention must be constantly kept up to their *forms*, that they do not lie in large stripes one beyond another; but that either they be quite intermingled, or, which is generally more pleasing, that considerable pieces of different tints, each a beautiful figure, be, in different proportions, placed near together. Exactness in the shapes must not be attempted, for it cannot be preserved; but if the great outlines be well drawn, little variations, afterwards occasioned by the growth of the plants, will not spoil them.

## XV.

A small thicket is generally most agreable, when it is one fine mass of well-mixed greens: that mass gives to the whole a *unity*, which can by no other means be so perfectly expressed. When more than one is necessary for the extent of the plantation, still if they are not too much contrasted, if the gradations from one to another are easy, the unity is not broken by the variety.

While the union of tints is productive of pleasing effects, strong effects may, on the other hand, be sometimes produced by their *disagreements*. Opposites, such, for instance, as the dark and light greens, in large quantities close together, break to pieces the surface upon which they meet; and an outline which cannot be sufficiently varied in form, may be in appearance, by the management of its shades: every opposition of tints is a break in a continued line: the depth of recesses may be deepened by darkening the greens as they retire; a tree which stands out from a plantation may be separated by its tint as much as by its position; the appearance of solidity or airiness in plants depends not solely on the thickness or thinness, but partly on the colour of the leaves; clumps at a distance, may be rendered more or less distinct by their greens; and the fine effect of a dark green tree, or groupe of trees, with nothing behind it but the splendor of a morning, or the glow of an evening sky, cannot be unknown to any who was ever delighted with a picture of Claude, or with the more beautiful originals in nature.

Another effect attainable by the aid of the different tints, is founded on the first principles of *perspective*. Objects grow faint as they retire from the eye; a detached clump, or a single tree of the lighter greens, will, therefore, seem farther off than one equidistant of a darker hue; and a regular gradation from one tint to another will alter the apparent length of a continued plantation, according as the dark or the light greens begin the gradation. In a strait line this is obvious; in a broken one, the fallacy in the appearance is seldom detected, only because the real extent is generally unknown; but experiments will support the principle, if they are made on plantations not very small, nor too close to the eye: the several parts may then be shortened or lengthened, and the variety of the outline be improved by a judicious arrangement of greens.

## XVI.

Other effects arising from mixtures of greens will occasionally present themselves in the *disposition* of a wood, which is the next consideration. Wood, as a general term, comprehends all trees and shrubs in whatever disposition; but it is specifically applied in a more limited sense, and in that sense I shall now use it.

Every plantation must be either a *wood*, a *grove*, a *clump*, or a *single tree*.

A wood is composed both of trees and underwood, covering a considerable space. A grove consists of trees without underwood; a clump differs from either only in extent; it may be either close or open; when close, it is sometimes called a *thicket*; when open, a *groupe of trees*; but both are equally clumps, whatever be the shape or situation.

## XVII.

One of the noblest objects in nature is the *surface of a large thick wood*, commanded from an eminence, or seen from below hanging on the side of a hill. The latter is generally the more interesting object; its aspiring situation gives it an air of greatness; its termination is commonly the horizon; and indeed if it is deprived of that splendid boundary, if the brow appears above it, (unless some very peculiar effect characterises that brow) it loses much of its magnificence; it is inferior to a wood which covers a less hill from the top to the bottom; for a whole space filled is seldom little: but a wood commanded from an eminence is generally no more than a part of the scene below; and its boundary is often inadequate to its greatness. To continue it, therefore, till it winds out of sight, or loses itself in the horizon, is generally desireable; but then the varieties of its surface grow confused as it retires; while those of a hanging wood are all distinct; the furthest parts are held up to the eye; and none are a distance, though the whole be extensive.

The varieties of a surface are essential to the beauty of it; a continued smooth shaven level of foliage is neither agreeable nor natural; the different growths of trees commonly break it in reality, and their shadows still more in appearance. These shades are so many tints, which undulating about the surface, are its greatest embellishment; and such tints may be produced with more effect, and more certainty, by a judicious mixture of greens; at the same time an additional variety may be introduced, by grouping and contrasting trees very different in shape from each other: and whether variety in the greens or in the forms be the design, the execution is often easy, and seldom to a certain degree impossible. In raising a young wood it may be perfect; in old woods there are many spots which may be either thinned or thickened; and there the characteristic distinctions should determine what to plant, or which to leave; at the least will often point out those which, as blemishes, ought to be taken away; and the removal of two or three trees will sometimes accomplish the design. The number of beautiful forms, and agreable masses, which may decorate the surface, is so great, that where the place will not admit of one, another is always ready; and as no delicacy of finishing is required, no minute exactness is worth regarding, great effects will not be disconcerted by small obstructions, and little disappointments.

The contrasts, however, of masses and of groupes must not be too strong, where *greatness* is the character of the wood; for unity is essential to greatness: and if direct opposites be placed close together, the wood is no longer one object; it is only a confused collection of several separate plantations; but if the progress be gradual from the one to the other, shapes and tints widely different may assemble on the same surface; and each should occupy a considerable space: a single tree, or a small cluster of trees, in the midst of an extensive wood, is in size but a speck, and in colour but a spot; the groupes and the masses must be large to produce any sensible variety.

Yet single trees in the midst of a wood, tho' seldom of use to diversify a surface, often deserve particular regard as individuals, and are important to the greatness of the whole. The superficies of a shrubby thicket, how extensive soever, does not convey the same ideas of magnificence, as that of a hanging wood; and yet at first sight, the difference is not always very discernible: it often requires time to collect the several circumstances in the latter, which suggest the elevation to which that broad expanse of foliage is raised, the vastness of the trunks which support it so high, the extent of the branches which spread it so far: when these circumstances, all of grandeur, croud together upon the mind, they dignify the space, which without them might indifferently be, the superficies of a thicket, or the surface of a wood: but a few large trees, not eminent above all about them, but distinguished by some slight separation, and obvious at a glance, immediately resolve the doubt; they are noble objects in themselves; become the situation; and serve as a measure to the rest. On the same principle, trees which are thin of boughs and of leaves, those whose branches tend upwards, or whose heads rise in slender cones, have an appearance more of airiness than of importance, and are blemishes in a wood where greatness is the prevailing idea. Those, on the contrary, whose branches hang directly down, have a breadth of head, which suits with such a situation, though their own peculiar beauty be lost in it.

These decorations are natural graces, which never derogate from greatness; and a number of shades playing on the surface, over a variety of those beautiful forms into which it may be cast, enliven that sameness, which, while it prevails, reduces the merit of one of the noblest objects in nature to that of mere space. To fill that space with objects of beauty; to delight the eye after it has been struck; to fix the attention where it has been caught; and to prolong astonishment into admiration, are purposes not unworthy of the greatest designs; and in the execution productive of embellishments, which in style are not unequal to scenes of richness and magnificence.

## XVIII.

When in a romantic situation, very broken ground is over-spread with wood, it may be proper on the surface of the wood, to mark the inequalities of the ground. *Rudeness*, not greatness, is the prevailing idea; and a choice directly the reverse of that which is productive of unity, will produce it; strong contrasts, even oppositions, may be eligible; the aim is rather to disjoint than to connect; a deep hollow may sink into dark greens; an abrupt bank may be shewn by a rising stage of aspiring trees; a sharp ridge by a narrow line of conical shapes: firs are of great use upon such occasions; their tint, their form, their singularity, recommend them.

A hanging *wood thin of forest trees*, and seen from below, is seldom pleasing: those few trees, are by the perspective brought near together; it loses the beauty of a thin wood, and is defective as a thick one; the most obvious improvement therefore is to thicken it. But when seen from an eminence, a thin wood is often a lively and elegant circumstance in a view; it is full of objects; and every separate tree shews its beauty. To increase that vivacity, which is the peculiar excellence of a thin wood, the trees should be characteristically distinguished both in their tints and their shapes; and such as for their airiness have been proscribed in a thick wood, are frequently the most eligible here. Differences also in their growths are a further source of variety; each should be considered as a distinct object, unless where a small number are grouped together; and then all that compose the little cluster must agree; but the groupes themselves, for the same reason as the separate trees, should be strongly contrasted; the continued underwood is their only connection; and that is not affected by their variety.

## XIX

Though the surface of a wood, when commanded, deserves all these attentions, yet the *outline* more frequently calls for our regard; it is also more in our power; it may sometimes be great, and may always be beautiful. The first requisite is irregularity. That a mixture of trees and underwood should form a long strait line, can never be natural; and a succession of easy sweeps and gentle rounds, each a portion of a greater or less circle, composing all together a line literally serpentine, is, if possible, worse. It is but a number of regularities put together in a disorderly manner, and equally distant from the beautiful both of art and of nature. The true beauty of an outline consists more in breaks than in sweeps; rather in angles than in rounds; in variety, not in succession.

The outline of a wood is a continued line, and small variations do not save it from the insipidity of sameness: one deep recess, one bold prominence, has more effect than twenty little irregularities. That one divides the line into parts, but no breach is thereby made in its unity; a continuation of wood always remains; the form of it only is altered, and the extent is encreased. The eye, which hurries to the extremity of whatever is uniform, delights to trace a varied line through all its intricacies, to pause from stage to stage, and to lengthen the progress. The parts must not, however, on that account be multiplied, till they are too minute to be interesting, and so numerous as to create confusion. A few large parts should be strongly distinguished in their forms, their directions, and their situations; each of these may afterwards be decorated with subordinate varieties; and the mere growth of the plants will occasion some irregularity; on many occasions more will not be required.

Every variety in the outline of a wood must be a *prominence*, or a *recess*. Breadth in either is not so important as length to the one, and depth to the other, If the former ends in an angle, the latter diminishes to a point, they have more force than a shallow dent, or a dwarf excrescence, how wide soever. They are greater deviations from the continued line which they are intended to break; and their effect is to enlarge the wood itself, which seems to stretch from the most advanced point, back beyond the most distant to which it retires. The extent of a large wood on a flat, not commanded, can by no circumstance be so manifestly shewn, as by a deep recess; especially if that recess wind so as to conceal the extremity, and leave the imagination to pursue it. On the other hand, the poverty of a shallow wood might sometimes be relieved by here and there a prominence, or clumps, which by their apparent junction should seem to be prominences from it. A deeper wood with a continued outline, except when commanded, would not appear so considerable.

An inlet into a wood seems to have been cut, if the opposite points of the entrance tally; and that shew of art depreciates its merit: but a difference only in the situation of those points, by bringing one more forward than the other, prevents the appearance, though their forms be similar. Other points, which distinguish the great parts, should in general be strongly marked; a short turn has more spirit in it than a tedious circuity; and a line broken by angles has a precision and firmness, which in an undulated line are wanting: the angles should indeed commonly be a little softened; the rotundity of the plant which forms them is sometimes sufficient for the purpose; but if they are mellowed down too much, they lose all meaning. Three or four large parts thus boldly distinguished, will break a very long outline; more may be, and often ought to be, thrown in, but seldom are necessary: and when two woods are opposed on the sides of a narrow glade, neither has so much occasion for variety in itself, as if it were single: if they are very different from each other, the contrast supplies the deficiency to each, and the interval between them is full of variety. The form of that interval is indeed of as much consequence as their own: though the outlines of both the woods be separately beautiful, yet if together they do not cast the open space into an agreable figure, the whole scene is not pleasing; and a figure is never agreable, when the sides too closely correspond; whether they are exactly the same, or exactly the reverse of each other, they equally appear artificial.

Every variety of outline hitherto mentioned, may be traced by the *underwood* alone; but frequently the same effects may be produced with more ease, and with much more beauty, by a *few trees* standing out from the thicket, and belonging, or seeming to belong to the wood, so as to make a part of its figure. Even where they are not wanted for that purpose, detached trees are such agreable objects, so distinct, so light, when compared to the covert about them, that skirting along it in some parts, and breaking it in others, they give an unaffected grace, which can no otherwise be given to the outline. They have a still further effect, when they stretch across the whole breadth of an inlet, or before part of a recess into the wood: they are themselves shewn to advantage by the space behind them, and that space, seen between their stems, they in return throw into an agreable perspective. An inferior grace of the same kind may be often introduced, only by distinguishing the boles of some trees in the wood itself, and keeping down the thicket beneath them. Where even this cannot be well executed, still the outline may be filled with such trees and shrubs as swell out in the middle of their growth, and diminish at both ends; or with such as rise in a slender cone; with those whose branches tend upwards; or whose base is very small in proportion to their height; or which are very thin of boughs and of leaves. In a confined garden scene, which wants room for the effect of detached trees, the outline will be heavy, if these little attentions are disregarded.

## XX.

The prevailing character of a wood is generally grandeur; the principal attention therefore which it requires, is to prevent the excesses of that character, to diversify the uniformity of its extent, to lighten the unwieldiness of its bulk, and to blend graces with greatness. But the character of a grove is *beauty*; fine trees are lovely objects; a grove is an assemblage of them; in which every individual retains much of its own peculiar elegance; and whatever it loses, is transferred to the superior beauty of the whole. To a grove, therefore, which admits of endless variety in the disposition of the trees, differences in their shapes and their greens are seldom very important, and sometimes they are detrimental. Strong contrasts scatter trees which are thinly planted, and which have not the connection of underwood; they no longer form one plantation; they are a number of single trees. A thick grove is not indeed exposed to this mischief, and certain situations may recommend different shapes and different greens for their effects upon the *surface*; but in the *outline* they are seldom much regarded. The eye attracted into the depth of the grove, passes by little circumstances at the entrance; even varieties in the form of the line do not always engage the attention: they are not so apparent as in a continued thicket, and are scarcely seen, if they are not considerable.

## XXI.

But the surface and the outline are not the only circumstances to be attended to. Though a grove be beautiful as an object, it is besides delightful as a spot to walk or to sit in; and the choice and the disposition of the trees for effects *within*, are therefore a principal consideration. Mere irregularity alone will not please: strict order is there more agreeable than absolute confusion; and some meaning better than none. A regular plantation has a degree of beauty; but it gives no satisfaction, because we know that the same number of trees might be more beautifully arranged. A disposition, however, in which the lines only are broken, without varying the distances, is less natural than any; for though we cannot find strait lines in a forest, we are habituated to them in the hedge rows of fields; but neither in wild nor in cultivated nature do we ever see trees equi-distant from each other: that regularity belongs to art alone. The distances therefore should be strikingly different; the trees should gather into groupes, or stand in various irregular lines, and describe several figures: the intervals between them should be contrasted both in shape and in dimensions: a large space should in some places be quite open; in others the trees should be so close together, as hardly to leave a passage between them; and in others as far apart as the connection will allow. In the forms and the varieties of these groupes, these lines, and these openings, principally consists the interior beauty of a grove.

The force of them is most strongly illustrated at Claremont*; where the walk to the cottage, though destitute of many natural advantages, and eminent for none; though it commands no prospect; though the water below it is a trifling pond; though it has nothing, in short, but inequality of ground to recommend it; is yet the finest part of the garden: for a grove is there planted in a gently curved direction, all along the side of a hill, and on the edge of a wood, which rises above it. Large recesses break it into several clumps, which hang down the declivity; some of them approaching, but none reaching quite to the bottom. These recesses are so deep as to form great openings in the midst of the grove; they penetrate almost to the covert; but the clumps being all equally suspended from the wood; and a line of open plantation, though sometimes narrow, running constant-

* Near Esher in Surry.

ly along the top; a continuation of grove is preserved, and the connection between the parts is never broken. Even a groupe, which near one of the extremities stands out quite detached, is still in stile so similar to the rest, as not to lose all relation. Each of these clumps is composed of several others still more intimately united; each is full of groupes, sometimes of no more than two trees; sometimes of four or five; and now and then in larger clusters: an irregular waving line, issuing from some little croud, loses itself in the next; or a few scattered trees drop in a more distant succession from the one to the other. The intervals, winding here like a glade, and widening there into broader openings, differ in extent, in figure, and direction; but all the groupes, the lines, and the intervals are collected together into large general clumps, each of which is at the same time both compact and free, identical and various. The whole is a place wherein to tarry with secure delight, or saunter with perpetual amusement.

The grove at Esher-place* was planted by the same masterly hand; but the necessity of accommodating the young plantation to some large trees which grew there before, has confined its variety. The groupes are few and small; there was not room for larger or for more: there were no opportunities to form continued narrow glades between opposite lines; the vacant spaces are therefore chiefly irregular openings spreading every way, and great differences of distance between the trees are the principal variety; but the grove winds along the bank of a large river, on the side and at the foot of a very sudden ascent, the upper part of which is covered with wood. In one place it presses close to the covert; retires from it in another; and stretches in a third across a bold recess, which runs up high into the thicket. The trees sometimes overspread the flat below; sometimes leave an open space to the river; at other times crown the brow of a large

* Contiguous to Claremont.

knole, climb up a steep, or hang on a gentle declivity. These varieties in the situation more than compensate for the want of variety in the disposition of the trees; and the many happy circumstances which concur

——————In Esher's peaceful grove,
Where Kent and nature vie for Pelham's love,

render this little spot more agreable than any at Claremont. But though it was right to preserve the trees already standing, and not to sacrifice great present beauties to still greater in futurity; yet this attention has been a restraint; and the grove at Claremont, considered merely as a plantation, is in delicacy of taste, and fertility of invention, superior to that at Esher.

Both were early essays in the modern art of gardening: and, perhaps from an eagerness to shew the effect, the trees in both were placed too near together: though they are still far short of their growth, they are run up into poles, and the groves are already past their prime; but the temptation to plant for such a purpose, no longer exists, now that experience has justified the experiment. If, however, we still have not patience to wait, it is possible to secure both a present and a future effect, by fixing first on a disposition which will be beautiful when the trees are large, and then intermingling another which is agreable while they are small. These occasional trees are hereafter to be taken away; and must be removed in time, before they become prejudicial to the others.

The consequence of variety in the disposition, is variety in the light and shade of the grove; which may be improved by the choice of the trees. Some are impenetrable to the fiercest sunbeam; others let in here and there a ray between the large masses of their foliage; and others, thin both of bough and of leaves, only chequer the ground. Every degree of light and shade, from a glare to obscurity, may be managed, partly by the number, and partly by the texture of the trees. Differences only in the manner of their growths have also corresponding effects; there is a closeness under those whose branches descend low, and spread wide; a space and liberty where the arch above is high; and frequent transition from the one to the other are very pleasing. These still are not all the varieties of which the interior of a grove is capable: trees indeed, whose branches nearly reach the ground, being each a sort of thicket, are inconsistent with an open plantation: but though some of the characteristic distinctions are thereby excluded, other varieties more minute succeed in their place; for the freedom of passage throughout brings every tree in its turn near to the eye, and subjects even differences in foliage to observation. These, slight as they may seem, are agreable when they occur: it is true they are not regretted, when wanting; but a defect of ornament is not necessarily a blemish.

## XXII.

It has been already observed, that clumps differ only in extent from woods, if they are close; or from groves, if they are open: they are small woods, and small groves, governed by the same principles as the larger, after allowances made for their dimensions. But besides the properties they may have in common with woods or with groves, they have others peculiar to themselves, which require examination.

They are either *independant* or *relative*; when independant, their beauty, as single objects, is solely to be attended to; when relative, the beauty of the individuals must be sacrificed to the effect of the whole, which is the greater consideration.

The least clump that can be, is of two trees; and the best effect they can have is, that their heads united should appear one large tree; two therefore of different species, or seven or eight of such shapes as do not easily join, can hardly be a beautiful groupe, especially if it have a tendency to a circular form. Such clumps of firs, though very common, are seldom pleasing; they do not compose one mass, but are only a confused number of pinnacles. The confusion is however avoided, by placing them in succession, not in clusters; and a clump of such trees is therefore more agreable when it is extended rather in length than in breadth.

Three trees together must form either a right line, or a triangle: to disguise the regularity, the distances should be very different. Distinctions in their shapes contribute also to the same end; and a variety in their growths still more. When a straight line consists of two trees nearly similar, and of a third much lower than they are, the even direction in which they stand is hardly discernible.

If humbler growths at the extremity can discompose the strictest regularity, the use of them is thereby recommended upon other occasions. It is indeed the variety peculiarly proper for clumps: every apparent artifice affecting the objects of nature, disgusts; and clumps are such distinguished objects, so liable to the suspicion of having been left or placed, on purpose to be so distinguished, that to divert the attention from these symptoms of art, irregularity in the composition is more important to them than to a wood or to a grove; being also less extensive, they do not admit so much variety of outline: but variety of growths is most observable in a small compass; and the several gradations may often be cast into beautiful figures.

The extent and the outline of a wood or a grove engage the attention more than the extremities; but in clumps these last are of the most consequence: they determine the form of the whole; and both of them are generally in sight: great care should therefore be taken to make them agreable and different. The ease with which they may be compared, forbids all similarity between them: for every appearance of equality suggests an idea of art; and therefore a clump as broad as it is long, seems less the

66

work of nature than one which stretches into length.

Another peculiarity of clumps, is the facility with which they admit a mixture of trees and of shrubs, of wood and of grove; in short, of every species of plantation. None are more beautiful than those which are so composed. Such compositions are, however, more proper in compact than in straggling clumps: they are most agreable when they form one mass: if the transitions from very lofty to very humble growths, from thicket to open to plantations, be frequent and sudden, the disorder is more suited to rude than to elegant scenes.

## XXIII.

The *occasions* on which independant clumps may be applied, are many. They are often desireable as beautiful objects in themselves; they are sometimes necessary to break an extent of lawn, or a continued line, whether of ground or of plantation; but on all occasions a jealousy of art constantly attends them, which irregularity in their figure will not always alone remove. Though elevations shew them to advantage, yet a hillock evidently thrown up on purpose to be crowned with a clump, is artificial to a degree of disgust; some of the trees should therefore be planted on the sides, to take off that appearance. The same expedient may be applied to clumps placed on the brow of a hill, to interrupt its sameness: they will have less ostentation of design, if they are in part carried down either declivity. The objection already made to planting many along such a brow, is on the same principle: a single clump is less suspected of art; if it be an open one, there can be no finer situation for it, than just at the point of an abrupt hill, or on a promontory into a lake or a river. It is in either a beautiful termination, distinct by its position, and enlivened by an expanse of sky or water, about and beyond it. Such advantages may balance little defects in its form; but they are lost if other clumps are planted near it: art then intrudes, and the whole is displeasing.

## XXIV.

But though a multiplicity of clumps, when each is an independant object, seldom seems natural; yet a number of them may, without any appearance of art, be admitted into the same scene, if they bear a *relation* to each other: if by their succession they diversify a continued outline of wood; if between them they form beautiful glades; if all together they cast an extensive lawn into an agreable shape, the *effect* prevents any scrutiny into the means of producing it. But when the reliance on that effect is so great, every other consideration must give way to the beauty of the whole. The figure of the glade, of the lawn, or of the wood, are principally to be attended to: the finest clumps, if they do not fall easily into the great lines, are blemishes; their connections, their contrasts are more important than their forms.

A line of clumps, if the intervals be closed by others beyond them, has the appearance of a wood, or of a grove; and in one respect the semblance has an advantage over the reality. In different points of view, the relations between the clumps are changed, and a variety of forms is produced, which no continued wood or grove, however broken, can furnish. These forms cannot all be equally agreable; and too anxious a sollicitude to make them every where pleasing, may, perhaps, prevent their being ever beautiful. The effect must often be left to chance; but it should be studiously consulted from a few principal points of view; and it is easy to make any recess, any prominence, any figure in the outline, by clumps thus advancing before, or retiring behind one another.

But amidst all the advantages attendant on this species of plantation, it is often exceptionable when commanded from a neighbouring eminence; clumps below the eye lose some of their principal beauties; and a number of them betray the art of which they are always liable to be suspected; they compose no surface of wood; and all effects arising from the relations between them are entirely lost. A prospect spotted with many clumps can hardly be great: unless they are so distinct as to be objects, or so distant as to unite into one mass, they are seldom an improvement of a view.

## XXV.

The proper situations for single trees are frequently the same as for clumps; the choice will often be determined, solely by the consideration of proportion, between the object, and the spot it is intended to occupy; and if the desired effect can be attained by a single tree, the simplicity of the means recommends it. Sometimes it will be preferred merely for variety; and may be used to mark one point in a scene in which two or three points are already distinguished by clumps. It may occasionally be applied to most of the purposes for which clumps are used; may be an independant object; may interrupt a continued line, or decorate an extent of space: there is but one effect resulting from clumps which may not to a certain degree be produced by single trees; a number of them will never unite into one large mass; but more distant relations may be observed between them. Scattered about a lawn, they may cast it into an agreable shape; and to produce that shape, each must be placed with an attention to the rest; they may stand in particular directions, and collectively form agreable figures; or between several straggling trees little glades may open, full of variety and beauty. The lines they trace, are fainter than those which larger plantations describe; but then their forms are their own, they are therefore absolutely free from all appearance of art; any disposition of them, if it be but irregular, is sure to be natural.

The situations of single trees is the first consideration; and differences in the distances between them their greatest variety. In shape, they admit of no choice but that which their species affords; greatness often, beauty often, sometimes mere solidity, and now and then peculiarity alone, recommends them. Their situations will also frequently determine the species: if they are placed before a continued line of wood only to break it, they should commonly be similar to the trees in that wood; they will else lose their connection, and not affect the outline which they are intended to vary; but if they are designed to be independant objects, they are as such more discernible when distinguished both in their shapes and their greens from any plantations about them. After all, the choice, especially in large scenes, is much confined to the trees on the spot; young clumps from the first have some, and soon produce a considerable effect; but a young single tree for many years has none at all; and it is often more judicious to preserve one already growing, tho' not exactly such as might be wished, either in itself, or in its situation, than to plant in its stead another, which may be a finer object, and better placed, in a distant futurity.

## Of WATER.

### XXVI.

In considering the subjects of gardening, ground and wood first present themselves; water is the next, which, though not absolutely necessary to a beautiful composition, yet occurs so often, and is so capital a feature, that it is always regretted when wanting; and no large place can be supposed, a little spot can hardly be imagined, in which it may not be agreable; it accommodates itself to every situation; is the most interesting object in a landscape, and the happiest circumstance in a retired recess; capti-

vates the eye at a distance, invites approach, and is delightful
when near; it refreshes an open exposure; it animates a shade;
chears the dreariness of a waste, and enriches the most crouded
view: in form, in style, and in extent, may be made equal to the
greatest compositions, or adapted to the least: it may spread in
a calm expanse to sooth the tranquility of a peaceful scene; or
hurrying along a devious course, add splendor to a gay, and extravagance to a romantic, situation. So various are the characters
which water can assume, that there is scarcely an idea in which
it may not concur, or an impression which it cannot enforce: a
deep stagnated pool, dank and dark with shades which it dimly
reflects, befits the seat of melancholy; even a river, if it be sunk
between two dismal banks, and dull both in motion and colour,
is like a hollow eye which deadens the countenance; and over a
sluggard, silent stream, creeping heavily along all together, hangs
a gloom, which no art can dissipate, nor even the sun-shine dis-
perse. A gently murmuring rill, clear and shallow, just gurgling,
just dimpling, imposes silence, suits with solitude, and leads to
meditation: a brisker current, which wantons in little eddies over
a bright sandy bottom, or babbles among pebbles, spreads chearfulness all around: a greater rapidity, and more agitation, to a
certain degree are animating; but in excess, instead of wakening,
they alarm the senses; the roar and the rage of a torrent, its force,
its violence, its impetuosity, tend to inspire terror; that terror
which, whether as cause or effect, is so nearly allied to sublimity.

Abstracted, however, from all these ideas, from every sensa-
tion, either of depression, composure, or exertion; and considering water merely as an object, no other is so apt soon to catch,
and long to fix the attention: but it may want beauties of which
we know it is capable; or the marks may be confused by which
we distinguish its species; and these defects displease: to avoid
them, the properties of each species must be determined.

All water is either *running*, or *stagnated*; when stagnated, it
forms a *lake* or a *pool*, which differ only in extent; and a *pool*

and a *pond* are the same. Running waters are either a *rivulet*, a *river* or a *rill*; and these differ only in breadth; as a *rivulet* and a *brook* are synonimous terms; a *stream* and a *current* are general names for all.

In a garden, the water is generally imitative. That which in the open country would be called a great pond, there assumes the name, and should be shaped as if it had the extent of a lake; for it is large in proportion to the other parts of the place. Though sometimes a real river passes through a garden, yet still but a small portion of it is seen; and more frequently the semblance only of such a portion is substituted instead of the reality. In either case, the imitation is lost, if the characteristic distinctions between a lake and a river be not scrupulously preserved.

## XXVII.

The characteristic property of running water is *progress*; of stagnated, is *circuity*: the one stretches into length; the other spreads over space: but it is not necessary that the whole circumference of a lake be seen, or that no bounds be set to the prospect of a river: on the contrary, the latter is never more beautiful than when it is lost in a wood, or retires behind a hill from the view: the former never appears so great as when its termination is concealed; the *shape*, not the *close*, denotes the character; if the opposite shores are both concave, they seem intended to surround, and to meet; if they are nearly parallel, they shew no tendency to come together, but suggest the idea of continuation.

To make both the banks of a river in concave forms is to sin against this first principle; and yet the fault is often committed, in order to encrease the expanse; but when the bold sweep of a river is thus converted into an insignificant pool, more is lost to the imagination in length, than is gained to the view in breadth; and, paradoxical as the assertion may seem, it is certainly true, that the water would appear more important, were it narrower. When one bank, therefore, retires, the other, if it does not advance, should, at the least, continue its former direction; or if that should be convex, it may be straitened; but both must not together depart from the appearance of progress.

Particular occasions may, however, justify a seeming deviation from the rule. To make room for an island, it may be proper to widen the river every way; for there the water is, in fact, intended to surround and to meet; while the currents on each side preserve the principal character. The same liberty may also be allowed on the influx of a collateral stream; and the accession will account both for the breadth and for the shape; but the licence must here be used with moderation, lest the wide place become principal, and divide the river into two streams, the one falling into a pool, and the other issuing from it. Both the sides of a lake may at all times retire; but on such an accession, the encrease should be chiefly on the shore opposite to the collateral stream, that it may appear to be a real enlargement of the lake, and not merely the mouth of a river.

A collateral stream should, in general, keep, or seem to keep for some way, to nearly the same breadth: if it diminishes very fast, it must soon come to an end, and has more the appearance of a creek than of a stream. Whether it be the one or the other, may be matter of indifference when it falls into a lake; but a creek is seldom agreable in a river; it diverts the current; its waters seem stagnated; it weakens the idea of progress.

All recesses in which the current is lost, are blemishes in a river; a bay is as exceptionable as a creek; whatever be the form, if it be a receptacle, not a passage, it is a symptom that the water rather spreads than proceeds, and hurts the character of the river: but a headland which only turns or contracts the stream, though it make a sort of bay, is not liable to the same objection. Such a bay has a vent; such an obstruction only strengthens the current; they do not suggest the most distant idea of stagnation. It is almost needless to add, that in a lake, just the reverse of a river, creeks, bays, recesses of every kind, are always in character, sometimes necessary, and generally beautiful: the objections to them in the one, are recommendations of them to the other.

## XXVIII.

Besides the circumstances which have been mentioned, and in which a river and a lake essentially differ; besides those in which they agree, and which are too obvious to require illustration; there are some peculiar to each character, and which, though common in the one, can hardly occur in the other; at least, not so often, nor to that degree, as to become subjects of comparison.

Space is essential to a lake; it may spread to any extent; and the mind, always pleased to expand itself on great ideas, delights even in its vastness. A lake cannot be too large as a subject of description, or of contemplation: but the eye receives little satisfaction when it has not a form on which to rest: the ocean itself hardly atones by all its grandeur for its infinity; and a prospect of it is, therefore, always most agreable, when in some part, at no great distance, a reach of shore, a promontory, or an island, reduces the immensity into shape. If the most extensive view which can be the object of vision, must be restrained in order to be pleasing; if the noblest ideas which the creation can suggest, must be checked in their career, before they can be reconciled to the principles of beauty; an offence against those principles, a transgression of that restraint, will not easily be forgiven on a subject less than infinite: a lake whose bounds are out of sight, is circumscribed in reality, not in appearance; at the same time that it disappoints the eye, it confines the imagination; it is but a waste of waters, neither interesting nor agreable.

A distant flat coast, dimly and doubtfully seen, does not obviate the objection; but it may be the means of removing it; for elevation and distinctness give an appearance of proximity, and contract the space they limit. This is the constant effect of a high shore; a low one, covered with wood, is in reality raised; and marked by buildings, becomes more conspicuous; it acquires an artificial elevation and distinctness.

These observations, though immediately relative to very large bodies of water, are still applicable to imitative lakes in parks and gardens. The principles upon which they are founded are equally true in both; and though an artificial lake cannot be supposed, which shall be absolutely, yet comparatively it may be extravagant: it may be so out of proportion to its appendages, as to seem a waste of water; for all size is in some respects relative: if this exceeds its due dimensions, and if a flatness of shore beyond it adds still to the dreariness of the scene, wood to raise the banks, and objects to distinguish them, will, from the same cause, produce the same effects as on a larger scale. If the length of a piece of water be too great for its breadth, so as to destroy all idea of circuity, the extremities should be considered as too far off, and made important, to give them proximity: while at the same time the breadth may be favoured, by keeping down the banks on the sides. On the same principle, if the lake be too small, a low shore will, in appearance, encrease the extent.

But it is not necessary that the whole scene be bounded: if form be impressed on a considerable part, the eye can, without disgust, permit a large reach to stretch beyond its ken; it can even be pleased to observe a tremulous motion in the horizon, which shews that the water has not there yet attained its termination. Still short of this, the extent may be kept in uncertainty; a hill or a wood may conceal one of the extremities, and the country beyond it, in such a manner, as to leave room for the supposed continuation of so large a body of water. Opportunities to choose this shape are frequent, and it is the most perfect of any: the scene is closed, but the extent of the lake is undetermined; a compleat form is exhibited to the eye, while a boundless range is left open to the imagination.

But mere form will only give content, not delight; that depends upon the outline, which is capable of exquisite beauty; and the *bays* and the *creeks*, and the *promontories*, which are ordinary parts of that outline, together with the accidents of *islands*, of *inlets* and of *outlets* to rivers, are in their shapes and their combinations an inexhaustible fund of variety.

A straight line of considerable length may find a place in that variety; and it is sometimes of singular use to prevent the semblance of a river in a channel formed between islands and the shore. But no figure perfectly regular ought ever to be admitted; it always seems artificial unless its size absolutely forbid the supposition. A semi-circular bay, though the shape be beautiful, is not natural; and any rectilinear figure is absolutely ugly; but if one line be curved, another may sometimes be almost straight; the contrast is agreable; and to multiply the occasions of shewing contrasts, may often be a reason for giving several directions to a creek, and more than two sides to a promontory.

Bays, creeks, and promontories, though extremely beautiful, should not, however, be very numerous; for a shore broken into little points and hollows has no certainty of outline; it is only ragged, not diversified; and the distinctness and simplicity of the great parts are hurt by the multiplicity of subdivisions: but islands, though the channels between them be narrow, do not so often derogate from greatness; they intimate a space beyond them whose boundaries do not appear; and remove to a distance the shore which is seen in perspective between them. Such partial interruptions of the sight suggest ideas of extent to the imagination.

The inlets and the outlets of rivers have similar effects: fancy pursues the course of the stream far beyond the view; no limits are fixed to its excursions. The greatest composition therefore of water is that, which is in part a lake, and in part a river; which has all the expanse of the one, and all the continuation of the other, each being strongly characterised to the very point of their junction: if that junction break into a side of the lake, the direction or the river should be oblique to the line it cuts; rectangular bisections are in this, as in all other instances, formal; but when the conflux is at an angle, so that the bank of the river coincides with one shore of the lake, they should both continue for some way in the same direction; a deviation from that line immediately at the outlet detaches the lake from the river.

## XXIX.

Though the windings of a river are proverbially descriptive of its course, yet without being perpetually wreathed, it may be natural; nor is the character expressed only by the turnings. On the contrary, if they are too frequent and sudden, the current is reduced into a number of separate pools, and the idea of progress is obscured by the difficulty of tracing it. Length is the strongest symptom of continuation; long reaches are, therefore, characteristic of a river, and they conduce much to its beauty; each is a considerable piece of water; and variety of beautiful forms may be given to their outlines; but a straight one can very seldom be admitted: it has the appearance of a cut canal, unless great breadth, a bridge across it, and strong contrasts between the objects on the banks, disguise the formality. A very small curvature obliterates every idea of art and stagnation; and a greater is often mischievous; for an excess of deviation from a straight towards a circular line, shortens the view, weakens the idea of continuation, and though not chargeable with stiffness, yet approaches to regularity; whereas the line of beauty keeps at a distance from every figure, which a rule can determine, or a compass describe.

A considerable degree of roundness is, however, often becoming, where the stream changes its direction; and if the turn be effected by a sharp point of land on one side, there is the more occasion for circuity on the other. The river should also be widened under that other bank; for it is the nature of water thus driven out of its course, to dash and encroach upon the opposite shore; where this circumstance has been attended to, the bend appears natural; and the view ending in space, gives scope to the imagination: the turn, therefore, ought generally to be larger than a right angle; if it be less, it closes immediately and checks the idea of progress.

## XXX.

To further that idea is one use of *bridges*; though they cross, they do not close the view: the water is seen to run through them, and is supposed to continue far beyond them; such a communication between the opposite banks implies the want of any other, and gives both length and depth to the stream. The form of a lake, on the contrary, intimates, that all the several shores are, by making a certain circuit, accessible. Bridges, therefore, are inconsistent with the nature of a lake, but characteristic of a river: they are on that account used to disguise a termination; but the deception has been so often practised, that it no longer deceives; and a bolder aim at the same effect will now be more successful. If the end can be turned just out of sight, a bridge at some distance raises a belief, while the water beyond it removes every doubt of the continuation of the river; the supposition immediately occurs, that if a disguise had been intended, the bridge would have been placed further back; and the disregard thus shewn to one deception, gains credit for the other.

To give to bridges their full effect, the connection between them and the river must be attended to: from the want of it, the

single wooden arch, now much in fashion, seems to me generally misplaced. Elevated without occasion so much above, it is
totally detached from the river; it is often seen straddling in
the air, without a glimpse of the water to account for it; and
the ostentation of it as an ornamental object, diverts all that
train of ideas which its use as a communication might suggest.
The vastness of Walton bridge cannot without affectation be
mimicked in a garden, where the magnificent idea of including
the Thames under one arch, is wanting; and where the structure itself, reduced to a narrow scale, retains no pretentions to
greatness. Unless the situation make such a height necessary: or
the point of view be greatly above it; or wood or rising ground,
instead of sky, behind it, fill up the vacancy of the arch; it seems
an effort without a cause, forced and preposterous.

The vulgar foot bridge, of planks only, guarded on one hand
by a common rail, and supported by a few ordinary piles, is
often more proper. It is perfect as a communication, because
it pretends to nothing further; it is the utmost simplicity of
cultivated nature: and if the banks from which it starts be of
a moderate heighth, its elevation preserves it from meanness.
No other species so effectually characterises a river; it seems too
plain for an ornament, too obscure for a disguise; it must be for
use; it can be a passage only; it is therefore spoiled, if adorned;
it is disfigured, if only painted of any other than a dusky colour.

But being thus incapable of all decoration and importance,
it is often too humble for a great, and too simple for an elegant
scene: a stone bridge is generally more suitable to either; but in
this also, an extraordinary elevation is seldom becoming, unless the grandeur compensate for the distance at which it leaves
the water below. A gentle rise, and easy sweep, more closely
preserve the relation: a certain degree of union should also be
formed between the banks and the bridge; that it may seem to
rise out of the banks, not barely to be imposed upon them. It
ought not generally to swell much above their level; the parapet

wall should be brought down near to the ground, or end against some swell; and the size and the uniformity of the abutments should be broken by hillocks or thickets about them: every expedient should be used to mark the connection of the building both with the ground from which it starts, and the water which it crosses.

In wild and romantic scenes may be introduced a ruined stone bridge, of which some arches may be still standing, and the loss of those which are fallen may be supplied by a few planks, with a rail, thrown over the vacancy. It is a picturesque object: it suits the situation; and the antiquity of the passage, the care taken to keep it still open, though the original building is decayed, the apparent necessity which thence results for a communication, give it an imposing air of reality.

In every scene of magnificence, in some where elegance chiefly prevails, a bridge with a colonade, or other ornamental structure upon it, is characteristically proper; and it has a peculiarity, which recommends it to many situations. The colonade is alone a perfect independent object, which may belong to several species of buildings; it may therefore embellish a scene where no water is visible; but the sight must not be let down below the balustrade. If the arches appear, this is like other bridges shewn by themselves; they may now and then be of use to mark a continuation of water, which would otherwise be doubtful; but in general they only remind us of what is wanting to the view.

In some situations, two or three bridges may be admitted into one scene; a collateral stream always, the turnings of the same stream often, afford opportunities to place them in several directions; and a greater distinction between objects is seldom required, than that between two bridges, in construction exactly alike, one of which presents the passage over it, and the other that under it, to the eye. Such a variety of beautiful forms have besides been invented for them, that in similar positions they may be objects in very different stiles: and collateral circumstances occasion still further distinctions. A bridge, which by means of a bend in the river is backed with wood or rising grounds, has in the effect little similarity to one, through which nothing can be seen, but the water and the sky; and if the accident which distinguishes immediately groupes with the bridge; if, for instance, a tree, or a little cluster of trees, stand so that the stems appear beneath, the heads above the arches, the whole is but one picturesque object, which retains no more than a distant resemblance to a bridge quite simple and unaccompanied. Amidst all this variety, two or three may easily be chosen, which in the same landscape, so far from assimilating, will diversify the parts; and, if properly disposed, neither in a confused croud, nor in a formal succession, will not incumber the view.

## XXXI.

A river requires a number of *accompaniments*; the changes in its course furnish a variety of situations; while the fertility, convenience, and amenity which attend it, account for all appearances of inhabitants and improvement. Profusion of ornament on a fictitious river, is a just imitation of cultivated nature; every species of building, every stile of plantation, may abound on the banks; and whatever be their characters, their proximity to the water is commonly the happiest circumstance in their situation. A lustre is from thence diffused on all around; each derives an importance from its relation to this capital feature; those which are near enough to be reflected, immediately belong to it; those at a greater distance still share in the animation of the scene; and objects totally detached from each other, being all attracted towards the same interesting connexion, are united into one composition.

In the front of Blenheim was a deep broad valley, which abruptly separated the castle from the lawn and the plantations before it; even a direct approach could not be made, without building a monstrous bridge over this vast hollow: but the forced communication was only a subject of raillery, and the scene continued broken into two parts, absolutely distinct from each other. This valley has been lately flooded; it is not filled; the bottom only is covered with water; the sides are still very high, but they are no longer the steeps of a chasm; they are the bold shores of a noble river. The same bridge is standing without alteration; but no extravagance remains; the water gives it propriety. Above it, the river first appears, winding from behind a small thick wood in the valley; and soon taking a determined course, it is then broad enough to admit an island filled with the finest trees; others corresponding to them in growth and disposition, stand in groupes on the banks, intermixed with younger plantations. Immediately below the bridge, the river spreads into a large expanse; the sides are open lawn; on that furthest from the house formerly stood the palace of Henry the Second, celebrated in many an ancient ditty by the name of fair Rosamond's Bower; a little clear spring which rises there is by the country people still called fair Rosamond's Well: the spot is now marked by a single willow. Near it is a fine collateral stream, of a beautiful form, retaining its breadth as far as it is seen, and retiring at last behind a hill from the view. The main river, having received this accession, makes a gentle bend, then continues for a considerable length in one wide direct reach, and, just as it disappears, throws itself down a high cascade, which is the present termination. On one of the banks of this reach is the garden; the steeps are there diversified with thickets and with glades; but the covert prevails, and the top is crowned with lofty trees. On the other side is a noble hanging wood in the park; it was depreciated when it sunk into a hollow, and was poorly lost in the bottom; but it is now a rich appendage to the river, falling down an easy slope quite to the water's edge, where, without overshadowing, it is reflected on the surface. Another face of the same wood borders the collateral stream, with an outline more indented and various; while a very large irregular clump adorns the opposite declivity. This clump is at a considerable distance from the principal river; but the stream it belongs to brings it down to connect with the rest; and the other objects, which were before dispersed, are now, by the interest of each in a relation which is common to all, collected into one illustrious scene. The castle is itself a prodigious pile of building, which, with all the faults in its architecture, will never seem less than a truly princely habitation; and the confined spot where it was placed, on the edge of an abyss, is converted into a proud situation commanding a beautiful prospect of water, and open to an extensive lawn, adequate to the mansion, and an emblem of its domain. In the midst of this lawn stands a column, a stately trophy, recording the exploits of the duke of Marlborough, and the gratitude of Britain. Between this pillar and the castle is the bridge, which now, applied to a subject worthy of it, is established in all the importance due to its greatness. The middle arch is wider than the Rialto, but not too wide for the occasion; and yet this is the narrowest part of the river: but the length of the reaches is every where proportioned to their breadth; each of them is alone a noble piece of water; and the last, the finest of all, loses itself gradually in a wood, which on that side is also the boundary of the lawn, and rises into the horizon. All is great in the front of Blenheim; but in that vast space no void appears, so important are the parts, so magnificent the objects: the plain is extensive; the valley is broad; the wood is deep; though the intervals between the buildings are large, they are filled with the grandeur, which buildings of such dimensions, and so much pomp, diffuse all around them; and the river in its long varied course, approaching to every object, and touching upon every part, spreads its influence over the whole. Notwithstanding their distances from each other, they all seem to be assembled about the water, which is every where a fine expanse, whose extremities are undetermined. In size, in form, and in stile, it is equal to the majesty of the scene; and is designed in the spirit, is executed with the liberality of the original donation, when this residence of a mighty monarch was bestowed by a great people, as a munificent reward on the hero who had deserved best of his country.

## XXXII.

In the composition of this scene, the river, both as a part itself, and as uniting the other parts, has a principal share; but water is not lost, though it be in so confined or so concealed a spot, as to enter into no view; it may render that spot delightful; it is capable of the most exquisite beauty in its form; and though not in space, may yet in disposition have pretensions to greatness; for it may be divided into several branches, which will form a cluster of islands all connected together, make the whole place irriguous, and in the stead of extent, supply a quantity of water. Such a sequestered scene usually owes its retirement to the trees and the thickets with which it abounds; but in the disposition of them, one distinction should be constantly attended to; a river flowing through a wood which overspreads one continued surface of ground, and a river between two woods, are in very different circumstances. In the latter case, the woods are separate; they may be contrasted in their forms and their characters; and the outline of each should be forcibly marked. In the former no outline ought to be discernible; for the river passes between trees, not between boundaries; and though in the progress of its course, the stile of the plantations may be often changed, yet on the opposite banks a similarity should constantly prevail, that the identity of the wood may never be doubtful.

A river between two woods may enter into a view; and then it must be governed by the principles which regulate the conduct and the accompaniments of a river in an open exposure; but when it runs through a wood, it is never to be seen in prospect; the place is naturally full of obstructions; and a continued opening, large enough to receive a long reach, would seem an artificial cut; the river must therefore necessarily wind more than in crossing a lawn, where the passage is intirely free: but its influence will never extend so far on the sides: the buildings must be near the banks; and, if numerous will seem crouded, being all in one track, and in situations nearly alike. The scene, however, does not want variety; on the contrary, none is capable of more: the objects are not indeed so different from each other as in an open view; but they are very different and in much greater abundance; for this is the interior of a wood, where every tree is an object; every combination of trees a variety; and no large intervals are requisite to distinguish the several dispositions; the grove, the thicket, or the groupes may prevail; and their forms and their relations may be constantly changed, without restraint of fancy, or limitation of number.

Water is so universally and so deservedly admired in a prospect, that the most obvious thought in the management of it, is to lay it as open as possible; and purposely to conceal it, would generally seem a severe self-denial: yet so many beauties may attend its passage through a wood, that larger portions of it might be allowed to such retired scenes, than are commonly spared from the view; and the different parts in different stiles would then be fine contrasts to each other. If the water at Wotton* were all exposed, a walk of near two miles along the banks would be of a tedious length, from the want of those changes of the scene, which now supply through the whole extent a succession of perpetual variety. That extent is so large as to admit of a division into four principal parts, all of them great in stile and in dimensions; and differing from each other both in character

* The seat of Mr. Grenville, in the vale of Aylesbury, in Buckinghamshire.

85

and situation. The two first are the least; the one is a reach of
a river, about the third of a mile in length, and of a competent
breadth, flowing through a lovely mead, open in some places
to views of beautiful hills in the country, and adorned in others
with clumps of trees, so large, that their branches stretch quite
across, and form a high arch over the water. The next seems to
have been once a formal basin, encompassed with plantations;
and the appendages on either side still retain some traces of
regularity; but the shape of the water is free from them; the size
is about fourteen acres; and out of it issue two broad collateral
streams, winding towards a large river, which they are seen to
approach, and supposed to join. A real junction is however impossible, from the difference of the levels; but the terminations
are so artfully concealed, that the deception is never suspected;
and when known is not easily explained. The river is the third
great division of the water; a lake into which it falls is the fourth.
These two do actually join; but their characters are directly opposite; the scenes they belong to are totally distinct; and the
transition from the one to the other is very gradual; for an island
near the conflux, dividing the breadth, and concealing the end
of the lake, moderates for some way the space; and permitting
it to expand but by degrees, raises an idea of greatness, from uncertainty accompanied with encrease. The reality does not disap-
point the expectation; and the island, which is the point of view,
is itself equal to the scene; it is large and high above the lake;
the ground is irregularly broken; thickets hang on the sides; and
towards the top is placed an Ionic portico, which commands
a noble extent of water, not less than a mile in circumference,
bounded on one side with wood, and open to the other to two
sloping lawns, the least of an hundred acres, diversified with
clumps, and bordered by plantations: yet this lake, when full in
view, and with all the importance which space, form, and situation can give, is not more interesting than the sequestered river,
which has been mentioned as the third great division of the

water. It is just within the verge of a wood, three quarters of a mile long, every where broad, and its course is such as to admit of infinite variety, without any confusion. The banks are cleared of underwood; but a few thickets still remain; and on one side an impenetrable covert soon begins; the interval is a beautiful grove of oaks, scattered over a green swerd of extraordinary verdure. Between these trees and these thickets the river seems to glide gently along, constantly winding, without one short turn, or one extended reach, in the whole length of the way. This even temper in the stream suits the scenes through which it passes; they are in general of a very sober cast; not melancholy, but grave; never exposed to a glare; never darkened with gloom; nor by strong contrasts of light and shade exhibiting the excess of either; undisturbed by an extent of prospects without, or a multiplicity of objects within, they retain at all times a mildness of character, which is still more forcibly felt when the shadows grow faint as they lengthen; when a little rustling of birds in the spray, the leaping of the fish, and the fragrancy of the woodbine, denote the approach of evening; while the setting sun shoots its last gleams on a Tuscan portico, which is close to the great basin, but which from a seat near this river is seen at a distance, through all the obscurity of the wood, glowing on the banks, and reflected on the surface of the water. In another still more distinguished spot is built an elegant bridge, with a colonade upon it, which not only adorns the place where it stands, but is also a picturesque object to an octagon building near the lake, where it is shewn in a singular situation, over-arched, encompassed, and backed with wood, without any appearance of the water beneath. This building in return is also an object from the bridge; and a Chinese room, in a little island just by, is another; neither of them are considerable; and the others which are visible are at a distance; but more or greater adventitious ornaments are not required in a spot so rich as this in beauties peculiar to its character. A profusion of water pours in from all sides round upon the view; the opening of the lake appears; a glimpse is caught of the large basin; one of the collateral streams is full in sight; and the bridge itself is in the midst of the finest part of the river; all seem to communicate the one with the other; though thickets often intercept, and groupes perplex the view, yet they never break the connection between the several pieces of water; each may still be traced along large branches, or little catches, which in some places are over-shadowed and dim; in others glisten through a glade, or glimmer between the boles of trees in a distant perspective; and in one, where they are quite lost to the view, some arches of a stone bridge, but partially seen among the wood, preserve their connection. However interrupted, however varied, they still appear to be parts of one whole, which has all the intricacy of number, and the greatness of unity; the variety of a stream, and the quantity of a lake; the solemnity of a wood, and the animation of water.

## XXXIII.

If a large river may sometimes, a smaller current undoubtedly may often, be conducted through a wood; it seldom adorns, it frequently disfigures a prospect, where its course is marked, not by any appearance of water, but by a confused line of clotted grass, which disagrees with the general verdure: a rivulet may, indeed, have consideration enough for a home scene, though it be open; but a rill is always most agreable when most retired from public view: its characteristic excellencies are vivacity and variety, which require attention, leisure, and silence, that the eye may pore upon the little beauties, and the ear listen to the low murmurs, of the stream, without interruption. To such indulgence a confined spot only is favourable; a close copse is, therefore, often more acceptable than a high wood; and a sequestered valley at all times preferable to any open exposure: a single rill at a very little distance is a mere water-course; it loses all its charms; it has no importance in itself, and bears no proportion to the scene. A number of little streams have, indeed, an effect in any situation, but not as objects; they are interesting only on account of the character they express; the irriguous appearance which they give to the whole.

The full tide of a large river has more force than activity, and seems too unwieldy to allow of very quick transitions; but in a rill, the agility of its motion accounts for every caprice; frequent windings disguise its insignificance; short turnings shew its vivacity; sudden changes in the breadth are a species of its variety; and however fantastically the channel may be wreathed, contracted, and widened, it still appears to be natural. We find an amusement in tracing the little stream through all the intricacies of its course, and in seeing it force a passage thro' a narrow streight, expatiate on every opportunity, struggle with obstructions, and puzzle out its way. A rivulet, which is the mean betwixt a river and a rill, partakes of the character of both: it is not licensed to the extravagance of the one, nor under the same restraints as the other; it may have more frequent bends than the river; longer reaches than a rill: the breadth of a stream determines whether the principal beauty results from extent or from variety.

The murmurs of a rill are amongst the most pleasing circumstances which attend it: if the bed of the stream be rough, mere declivity will occasion a constant ripling noise; when the current drops down a descent, though but of a few inches, or forcibly bubbles up from a little hollow, it has a deep gurgling tone, not uniformly continued, but incessantly repeated, and therefore more engaging than any; the flattest of all, is that found rather of the splashing than the fall of water, which an even gentle slope, or a tame obstruction, will produce; this is less pleasing than the others; but none should be entirely excluded; all in their turns are agreable; and the choice of them is much in our power; by observing their causes, we may often find the means to strengthen, to weaken, or to change them; and the addition or removal of a single stone, or a few pebbles, will sometimes be sufficient for the purpose.

## XXXIV.

A rill cannot pretend to any sound beyond that of a little water-fall: the roar of a cascade belongs only to larger streams; but it may be produced by a rivulet to a considerable degree; and attempts to do more have generally been unsuccessful: a vain ambition to imitate nature in her great extravagancies betrays the weakness of art: though a noble river, throwing itself head-long down a precipice be an object truly magnificent; it must, however, be confessed, that in a single sheet of water there is a formality, which its vastness alone can cure; but the heighth not the breadth is the wonder; when it falls no more than a few feet, the regularity prevails; and its extent only serves to expose the vanity of affecting the style of a cataract in an artificial cascade; it is less exceptionable if divided into several parts; for then each separate part may be wide enough for its depth; and in the whole, variety, not greatness, will be the predominant character: but a structure of rough, large, detached, stones, cannot easily be contrived of strength sufficient to support a great weight of water; it is sometimes from necessity almost smooth and uniform; and then it loses much of its effect; several little falls in succession are preferable to one great cascade which in figure or in motion approaches to regularity.

When greatness is thus reduced to number, and length becomes of more importance than breadth, a rivulet vies with a river; and it more frequently runs in a continued declivity, which is very favourable to such a succession of falls. Half the expence and labour which are sometimes bestowed on a river, to give it, at the best, a forced precipitancy, in one spot only, would animate a rivulet through the whole of its course; and after all, the most interesting circumstance in falling waters is their animation; a great cascade fills us with surprise; but all surprise must cease: and the motion, the agitation, the rage, the froth, and the variety of the water, are finally the objects which engage the attention: for these a rivulet is sufficient; and they may there be produced without that appearance of effort which raises a suspicion of art.

To obviate such a suspicion, it may be sometimes expedient to begin the descent out of sight; for the beginning is the difficulty; if that be concealed, the subsequent falls seem but a consequence of the agitation which characterises the water at its first appearance; and the imagination is, at the same time, let loose to give ideal extent to the cascades: when a stream issues from a wood, such management will have a great effect: the bends of its course in an open exposure may afford frequent opportunities for it: and sometimes a low broad bridge may furnish the occasion; a little fall hid under the arch will create a disorder, in consequence of which, a greater cascade below will appear very natural.

## Of ROCKS.

### XXXV.

Rills, rivulets, and cascades, abound among rocks; they are natural to the scene; and such scenes commonly require every *accompaniment* which can be procured for them: mere rocks, unless they are peculiarly adapted to certain impressions, may surprise, but can hardly please; they are too far removed from common life, too barren, and unhospitable; rather desolate than solitary, and more horrid than terrible; so austere a character cannot be long engaging, if its rigour be not softened by circumstances, which may belong either to these or to more cultivated spots; and when the dreariness is extreme, little streams and water-falls are of themselves insufficient for the purpose; an intermixture of vegetation is also necessary; and on some occasions even marks of inhabitants are proper.

*Middleton dale is a cleft between rocks, ascending gradually from a romantic village, till it emerges, at about two miles distance, on the vast moor-lands of the Peake; it is a dismal entrance to a desart; the hills above it are bare; the rocks are of a grey colour; their surfaces are rugged; and their shapes savage; frequently terminating in craggy points; sometimes resembling vast unwieldy bulwarks; or rising in heavy buttresses, one above another; and here and there a mishapen mass bulging out hangs lowering over its base. No traces of men are to be seen, except in a road which has no effect on such a scene of desolation; and in the lime kilns constantly smoaking on the side; but the labourers who occasionally attend them live at a distance; there is not a hovel in the dale; and some scanty withering bushes are all its vegetation; for the soil between the rocks produces as little as they do; it is disfigured with all the tinges of brown and red, which denote barrenness; in some places it has crumbled away, and strata of loose dark stones only appear: and in others, long lines of dross and rubbish shoveled out of mines, have fallen down the steeps. In these mines, the veins of lead on one side of the dale, are observed always to have corresponding veins, in exactly in the same direction, on the other: and the rocks, though differing widely in different places, yet always continue in one style for some way together, and seem to have a relation to each other; both these appearances make it probable, that Middleton dale is a chasm rent in the mountain by some convulsion of nature, beyond the memory of man,

* Near Chatsworth.

or perhaps before the island was peopled: the scene, though it does not prove the fact, yet justifies the supposition; and it gives credit to the tales of the country people, who, to aggravate its horrors, always point to a precipice, down which they say, that a poor girl of the village threw herself headlong, in despair, at the neglect of the man whom she loved: and shew a cavern, where a skeleton was once discovered; but of what wretch is unknown; his bones were the only memorial left of him: all the dreariness however of the place, which accords so well with such traditions, abates upon the junction of another valley, the sides of which are still of rock, but mixed and crowned with fine wood; and Middleton dale becomes more mild by sharing in its beauties: near this junction a clear stream issues from under the hill, and runs down the dale, receiving as it proceeds many rills and springs, all as transparent as itself: the principal rivulet is full of little water-falls; they are sometimes continued in succession along a reach of considerable length, which is whitened with froth all the way; at other times the brook wreathes in frequent windings, and drops down a step at every turn; or slopes between tufts of grass, in a brisk, though not a precipitate descent; when it is most quiet, a thousand dimples still mark its vivacity; it is every where active; sometimes rapid; seldom silent; but never furious or noisy: the first impressions which it makes are of sprightliness and gaiety, very different from those which belong to the scene all around; but by dwelling upon both, they are brought nearer together; and a melancholy thought occurs, that such a stream should be lost in watering a waste; the wilderness appears more forlorn which so much vivacity cannot enliven: as the idea of desolation is heightened by reflecting that the

> Flower is born to blush unseen,
> And waste its sweetness on the desart air.

And that

> The nightingale attunes her notes,
> Where none are left to hear.

If such a scene occurs within the precincts of a park or a garden, no expence should be spared to meliorate the soil, wherever any soil can be found: without some vegetation among the rocks, they are only an object of curiosity, or a subject of wonder; but verdure alone will give some relief to the dreariness of the scene; and shrubs or bushes, without trees, are a sufficiency of wood; the thickets may also be extended by the creeping plants, such as pyracantha, vines, and ivy, to wind up the sides, or cluster on the tops of the rocks; and to this vegetation may be added some symptoms of inhabitants, but they must be slight and few; the use of them is only to cheer, not to destroy the solitude of the place; and such therefore should be chosen as are sometimes found in situations retired from publick resort; a cottage may be lonely; but it must not here seem ruinous and neglected; it should be tight and warm, with every mark of comfort about it, to which its position in some sheltered recess may greatly contribute. A cavity also in the rocks, rendered easy of access, improved to a degree of convenience, and maintained in a certain state of preservation, will suggest similar ideas of protection from the bitterest inclemencies of the sky, and even of occasional refreshment and repose; but we may venture still further; a mill is of necessity often built at some distance from the town which it supplies; and here it would at the same time apply the water to a use, and encrease its agitation. The dale may besides be made the haunt of those animals, such as goats, which are sometimes wild, and sometimes domestic; and which accidentally appearing, will divert the mind from the sensations, natural to the scene, but not agreable if continued long without interruption. These and such other expedients, will approximate the severest retreat to the habitations of men, and convert the appearance of a perpetual banishment, into that of a temporary retirement from society.

But too strong a force on the nature of the place always fails; a winding path, which appears to be worn, not cut, has more effect than a high road, all artificial and level, which is too weak to overbear, and yet contradicts the general idea: the objects therefore to be introduced must be those which hold a mean between solitude and population; and the inclination of that choice towards either extreme, should be directed by the degree of wildness which prevails; for though that runs sometimes to an excess which requires correction; at other times it wants encouragement; and at all times it ought to be preserved: it is the predominant character of rocks, which mixes with every other, and to which all the appendages must be accommodated; and they may be applied, so as greatly to encrease it: a licentious irregularity of wood and of ground, and a fantastic conduct of the streams, neither of which would be tolerated in the midst of cultivation, become and improve romantic spots; even buildings, partly by their style, but still more by their position, in strange, difficult, or dangerous situations, distinguish and aggravate the native extravagancies of the scene.

In the choice and the application of these accompaniments, consists all our power over rocks; they are themselves too vast and too stubborn to submit to our controul; but by the addition or removal of the appendages, which we can command, parts may be shewn or concealed, and the characters with their impressions may be weakened or enforced: to adapt the accompaniments accordingly, is the utmost ambition of art when rocks are the subject.

Their most distinguished characters are, *dignity*, *terror* and *fancy*: the expressions of all are constantly wild; and sometimes a rocky scene is only wild, without pretensions to any particular character.

## XXXVI.

That which inspires ideas of greatness, as distinguished from those of terror, has less wildness in it than any; there is a composure in dignity, which is disconcerted by quick transitions, and the flutter of variety; a succession therefore of nearly the same forms, a repetition of them one above the other, do not derogate from an effect, which depends more on the extent than the changes of the scene: the dimensions which are necessary to produce that effect, contract the room for variety; the parts must be large; if the rocks are only high, they are but stupendous not majestic: breadth is equally essential to their greatness; and every slender, every grotesque shape, is excluded.

Art may interpose to shew these large parts to the eye, and magnify them to the imagination, by taking away thickets which stretch quite across the rocks, so as to disguise their dimensions; or by filling with wood the small intervals between them; and thus by concealing the want, preserving the appearance of continuation.

When rocks retire from the eye down a gradual declivity, we can, by raising the upper ground deepen the fall, lengthen the perspective, and give both height and extent to those at a distance: this effect may be still encreased by covering that upper ground with a thicket, which shall cease, or be lowered, as it descends.

A thicket, on other occasions, makes the rocks which rise out of it seem larger than they are; if they stand upon a bank overspread with shrubs, their beginning is at the least uncertain; and the presumption is, that they start from the bottom.

Another use of this brushy underwood is to conceal the fragments and rubbish which have fallen from the sides and the brow, and which are often unsightly. Rocks are seldom remarkable for the elegance of their forms; they are too vast, and too rude, to pretend to delicacy; but their shapes are often agreable;

and we can affect those shapes to a certain degree, at least we can cover many blemishes in them, by conducting the growth of shrubby and creeping plants about them.

For all these purposes mere underwood suffices; but for greater effects larger trees are requisite; they are worthy of the scene; and not only improvements, but accessions to its grandeur; we are used to rank them among the noblest objects of nature; and when we see that they cannot aspire to the midway of the heights around them, the rocks are raised by the comparison. A single tree is, therefore, often preferable to a clump; the size, though really less, is more remarkable: and clumps are besides generally exceptionable in a very wild spot, from the suspicion of art which attends them; but a wood is free from that suspicion; and its own character of greatness recommends it to every scene of magnificence.

On the same principle, all the consideration which can be, should be given to the streams; no number of little rills are equal to one broad river; and in the principal current, some varieties may be sacrificed to importance; but a degree of strength should always be preserved; the water, though it needs not be furious should not be dull; for dignity, when most serene, is not languid; and space will hardly atone for want of animation.

The character, however, of greatness, when divested of terror, is placid; it does not, therefore, exclude marks of inhabitants, though it never requires them to tame its wildness; and without inviting, it occasionally admits an intermixture of vegetation; it even allows of buildings intended only to decorate the scene; but they must be adequate to it, both in size and in character: and if cultivation is introduced, that too should be conformable to the rest; not a single narrow patch cribbed out of the waste; but the confines of a country shelving into the vale, and suggesting the idea of extent; nothing trivial ought to find admittance; but on the other hand, the character is not violated by a mixture of agreableness with its grandeur; and far less is extravagance required to support it: strange shapes in extraordinary positions; enormous weights unaccountably sustained; trees rooted in the sides, and torrents raging at the foot, of the rocks, are, at the best needless excesses: there is a temperance in dignity, which is rather hurt by a wanton violence on the common order of nature; great objects alone, great in their dimensions and in their style, are amply sufficient to satisfy and to fill the mind; when these fail, then, and then only, we are apt to have recourse to wonder, in order to excite admiration.

Many of the circumstances which have been mentioned concur at *Matlock Bath, which is situated in a vale near three miles long, shut up at one end by a rising moor, and at the other end by vast cliffs of rock: the entrance into it is hewn through one of them, and is indeed a noble rude portal to a scene of romantic magnificence. One side of the valley is a very high range of hill, rough with bushes, and great blocks or ledges of stone; the other side is washed by the Derwent, and chiefly of rocks; which, however, are often interrupted by steep declivities of greenswerd, large thickets, and gentle descents of fine fields from the adjacent country. The rocks sometimes form the brow, sometimes they fix the foot, and sometimes they break the sides of the hill; at the high Tor they are an hundred and twenty three yards above the water; in other places they are no more than an abrupt bank of a few feet to the river; for the most part they are nearly perpendicular, falling in several stages, or in one vast precipice from the top to the bottom; but though similar in shape, they are widely different in their construction; in one place they are irregularly jointed; in another more uniformly ribbed; in a third they form a continued surface from the summit to the base; and frequently they are composed of enormous masses of stone

*    In Derbyshire.

heaped upon each other. From some such scene probably
was conceived the wild imagination in antient mythology of
the giants piling Pelion upon Ossa: in this, all is vast; height,
breadth, solidity, boldness of idea, and unity of style, combine
to form a character of greatness, consistent throughout, not
uniform, unmixed with any littleness, unallayed with any extravagance. The colour of the rocks is almost white; and their
splendor is enhanced in many places by ivy and single yew
trees appearing amongst them: the intervals between them are
generally filled with a brushy underwood, which diversifies
and embellishes the scene very beautifully; but for want of
large trees adds nothing to its grandeur; there are few of any
note through out the vale; the best are in a small wood near
the bath; but they are not adequate to the magnificence of the
objects around them, to the steeps of the hill, the loftiness of
the rocks, and the character of the Derwent. That character
is, indeed, rather too strong for the place: in size, and in the
direction of its course, the river is exactly such as might be
wished; but it is a torrent, in which force and fury prevail; the
cascades in it are innumerable; before the water is recovered
from one fall, it is hurried down another; and its agitation
being thus encreased by repeated shocks, it pushes on with
restless violence to the next, where it dashes against fragments
of rocks, or foams among heaps of stones which the stream
has driven together. The colour all along is of a reddish brown;
even the foam is tinged with a dusky hue: and where there are
no cascades, still the declivity of the bed preserves the rapidity,
and a quantity of little breakers continue the turbulence of the
current. Many of these circumstances are certainly great; but
a more temperate river, rolling its full tide along with strength
and activity, without rage; falling down one noble cascade,
instead of many; and if animated sometimes by resistance, yet
not constantly struggling with obstructions, would have been
more consistent with the sedate steady dignity of these noble

piles of rock, whose brightness, together with the verdure of a vigorous and luxuriant, though humble vegetation, and some appearances of culture, give to the whole an air of chearful serenity, which is disturbed by the impetuosity of the Derwent.

## XXXVII.

This river would be better suited to a scene characterised by that terror, which the combination of greatness with force inspires, and which is animating and interesting, from the exertion and anxiety attending it. The terrors of a scene in nature are like those of a dramatic representation; they give an alarm; but the sensations are agreable, so long as they are kept to such as are allied only to terror, unmixed with any that are horrible and disgusting; art may therefore be used to heighten them, to display the objects which are distinguished by greatness, to improve the circumstances which denote force, to mark those which intimate danger, and to blend with all, here and there a cast of melancholy.

Greatness is as essential to the character of terror as to that of dignity; vast efforts in little objects are but ridiculous; nor can force be supposed upon trifles incapable of resistance; on the other hand it must be allowed, that exertion and violence supply some want of space; a rock wonderfully supported, or threatening to fall, acquires a greatness from its situation, which it has not in dimensions; so circumstanced, the size appears to be monstrous: a torrent has a consequence which a placid river of equal breadth cannot pretend to; and a tree which would be inconsiderable in the natural soil, becomes important when it bursts forth from a rock.

Such circumstances should be always industriously sought for; it may be worth while to cut down several trees, in order to exhibit one apparently rooted in the stone. By the removal perhaps of only a little brush wood, the alarming disposition of a rock, strangely undermined, rivetted, or suspended, may be shewn; and if there be any soil above its brow, some trees planted there, and impending over it, will make the object still more extraordinary. As to the streams, great alterations may generally be made in them; and therefore it is of use to ascertain the species proper to each scene, because it is in our power to enlarge or contract their dimensions; to accelerate or retard their rapidity; to form, encrease, or take away obstructions; and always to improve, often to change, their characters.

Inhabitants furnish frequent opportunities to strengthen the appearances of force, by giving intimations of danger. A house placed at the edge of a precipice, any building on the pinnacle of a crag, makes that situation seem formidable, which might otherwise have been unnoticed; a steep, in itself not very remarkable, becomes alarming, when a path is carried aslant up the side; a rail on the brow of a perpendicular fall, shews that the height is frequented and dangerous; and a common foot-bridge thrown over a cleft between rocks, has a still stronger effect. In all these instances, the imagination immediately transports the spectator to the spot, and suggests the idea of looking down such a depth; in the last, that depth is a chasm, and the situation is directly over it.

In other instances, exertion and danger seem to attend the occupations of the inhabitants;

——— Half way down
Hangs one that gathers samphire; dreadful trade!

is a circumstance chosen by the great master of nature, to aggravate the terror of the scene he describes. Mines are frequent in rocky places; and they are full of ideas suited to such occasions. To these may sometimes be added the operations of engines; for machinery, especially when its powers are stupendous, or its effects formidable, is an effort of art, which may be accommodated to the extravagancies of nature.

A scene at the *New Weir on the Wye, which in itself is truly great and awful, so far from being disturbed, becomes more interesting and important, by the business to which it is destined. It is a chasm between two high ranges of hill, which rise almost perpendicularly from the water; the rocks on the sides are mostly heavy masses; and their colour is generally brown; but here and there a pale craggy shape starts up to a vast height above the rest, unconnected, broken, and bare: large trees frequently force out their way amongst them; and many of them stand far back in the covert, where their natural dusky hue is deepened by the shadow which overhangs them. The river too, as it retires, loses itself in woods which close immediately above, then rise thick and high, and darken the water. In the midst of all this gloom is an iron forge, covered with a black cloud of smoak, and surrounded with half-burned ore, with coal, and with cinders; the fuel for it is brought down a path, worn into steps narrow and steep, and winding among precipices; and near it is an open space of barren moor, about which are scattered the huts of the workmen. It stands close to the cascade of the Weir, where the agitation of the current is encreased by large fragments of rocks, which have been swept down by floods from the banks, or shivered by tempests from the brow; and the sullen sound, at stated intervals, from the strokes of the great hammers in the forge, deadens the roar of the water-fall. Just below it, while the rapidity of the stream still continues, a ferry is carried across it; and lower down the fishermen use little round boats, called truckles, the remains perhaps of the ancient British navigation, which the least motion will overset and the slightest touch may destroy. All the employments of the people seem

* Near a place called Symond's Gate, between Ross and Monmouth.

to require either exertion or caution; and the ideas of force or of danger which attend them, give to the scene an animation unknown to a solitary, though perfectly compatible with the wildest romantic situations.

But marks of inhabitants must not be carried to the length of cultivation, which is too mild for the ruggedness of the place, and has besides an air of chearfulness inconsistent with the character of terror; a little inclination towards melancholy is generally acceptable, at least to the exclusion of all gaiety; and beyond that point, so far as to throw just a tinge of gloom upon the scene. For this purpose, the objects whose colour is obscure should be preferred; and those which are too bright may be thrown into shadow; the wood may be thickened, and the dark greens abound in it; if it is necessarily thin, yews and shabby firs should be scattered about it; and sometimes to shew a withering or a dead tree, it may for a space be cleared entirely away. All such circumstances are acquisitions, if they can be had without detriment to the principal character; for it must ever be remembered, that where terror prevails, melancholy is but a secondary consideration.

## XXXVIII.

The different species of rocks often meet in the same place, and compose a noble scene, which is not distinguished by any particular character; it is only when one eminently prevails, that it deserves such a preference as to exclude every other. Sometimes a spot, remarkable for nothing but its wildness, is highly romantic; and when this wildness rises to fancy, when the most singular, the most opposite forms and combinations are thrown together, then a mixture also of several characters adds to the number of instances which there concur to display the inexhaustible variety of nature.

So much variety, so much fancy, are seldom found within the same extent as in Dovedale*; it is about two miles in length, a deep, narrow, hollow valley; both the sides are of rock; and the Dove in its passage between them is perpetually changing its course, its motion, and appearance. It is never less than ten, nor so much as twenty yards wide, and generally about four feet deep; but transparent to the bottom, except when it is covered with a foam of the purest white, under water-falls which are perfectly lucid: these are very numerous, but very different; in some places they stretch strait across, or aslant the stream; in other they are only partial; and the water either dashes against the stones, and leaps over them; or pouring along a steep, re-bounds upon those below; sometimes it rushes through the sev-eral openings between them; sometimes it drops gently down; and at other times it is driven back by the obstruction, and turns into an eddy. In one particular spot, the valley almost clos-ing, leaves hardly a passage for the river, which pent up, and struggling for a vent, rages, and roars and foams, till it has ex-tricated itself from the confinement. In other parts, the stream, tho' never languid, is often gentle; flows round a little desart island, glides between aits of bulrushes, disperses itself among tufts of grass or of moss, bubbles about a water-dock, or plays with the slender threads of aquatic plants which float upon the surface. The rocks all along the dale vary as often in their structure, as the stream in its motion; in one place an extended surface gradually diminishes from a broad base almost to an edge; in another, a heavy top hanging forwards, overshadows all beneath; sometimes many different shapes are confusedly tumbled together; and sometimes they are broken into slender sharp pinnacles, which rise upright, often two or three together, and often in more numerous clusters. On this side of the dale, they are universally bare; on the other, they are intermixed with

* Near Ashbourne in Derbyshire.

wood; and the vast height of both the sides, with the narrowness of the interval between them, produces a further variety; for whenever the sun shines from behind the one, the form of it is distinctly and completely cast upon the other; the rugged surface on which it falls diversifies the tints; and a strong reflected light often glares on the edge of the deepest shadow. The rocks never continue long in the same figure or situation, and are very much separated from each other: sometimes they form the sides of the valley, in precipices, in steeps, or in stages; sometimes they seem to rise in the bottom, and lean back against the hill; and sometimes they stand out quite detached, heaving up in cumbrous piles, or starting into conical shapes, like vast spars, an hundred feet high; some are firm and solid throughout; some are cracked; and some, split and undermined, are wonderfully upheld by fragments apparently unequal to the weight they sustain. One is placed before, one over another, and one fills at some distance behind an interval between two. The changes in their disposition are infinite; every step produces some new combination; they are continually crossing, advancing, and retiring: the breadth of the valley is never the same forty yards together; at the narrow pass which has been mentioned, the rocks almost meet at the top, and the sky is seen as through a chink between them: just by this gloomy abyss, is a wider opening, more light, more verdure, more chearfulness, than any where else in the dale. Nor are the forms and the situations of the rocks their only variety; many of them are perforated by large natural cavities; some of which open to the sky; some terminate in dark recesses; and through some are to be seen several more uncouth arches, and rude pillars, all detached, and retiring beyond each other, with the light shining in between them, till a rock far behind them closes the perspective: the noise of the cascades in the river echoes amongst them; the water may often be heard at the same time gurgling near, and roaring at a distance; but no other sounds disturb the silence of the spot; the only trace of men is a blind path, but lightly and but seldom trodden, by those whom curiosity leads to see the wonders they have been told of Dovedale. It seems, indeed, a fitter haunt for more ideal beings; the whole has the air of enchantment; the perpetual shifting of the scenes; the quick transitions; the total changes; then the forms all around, grotesque as chance can cast, wild as nature can produce, and various as imagination can invent; the force which seems to have been exerted to place some of the rocks where they are now fixed immoveable; the magick by which others appear still to be suspended; the dark caverns; the illuminated recesses; the fleating shadows, and the gleams of light glancing on the sides, or trembling on the stream; and the loneliness and the stillness of the place, all crouding together on the mind almost realize the ideas which naturally present themselves in this region of romance and of fancy.

The solitude of such a scene is agreable, on account of the endless entertainment which its variety affords, and in the contemplation of which both the eye and the mind are delighted to indulge: marks of inhabitants and cultivation disturb that solitude; and ornamental buildings are too artificial in a place so absolutely free from restraint. The only accompaniments proper for it are wood and water; and by these sometimes improvements may be made: when two rocks similar in shape and position are near together, by skirting one of them with wood, while the other is left bare, a material distinction is established between them; if the streams be throughout of one character, it is in our power, and should be our aim, to introduce another. Variety is the peculiar property of the spot, and every accession to it is a valuable acquisition. On the same principle, endeavours should be used not only to multiply, but to aggravate differences, and to encrease distinctions into contrasts: but the subject will impose a caution against attempting too much. Art must almost despair of improving a scene, where nature seems to have exerted her invention.

## Of BUILDINGS.

## XXXIX.

Buildings are the very reverse of rocks. They are absolutely in our power, both the species and the situation; and hence arises the excess in which they often abound. The desire of doing something is stronger than the fear of doing too much: these may always be procured by expence, and bought by those who know not how to choose; who consider profusion as ornament; and confound by number, instead of distinguishing by variety.

Buildings probably were first introduced into gardens merely for convenience, to afford refuge from a sudden shower, and shelter against the wind; or, at the most, to be seats for a party, or for retirement: they have since been converted into objects, and now the original *use* is too often forgotten in the greater purposes to which they are applied; they are considered as objects only, the inside is totally neglected; and a pompous edifice frequently wants a room barely comfortable. Sometimes the pride of making a lavish display to a visitor, without any regard to the owner's enjoyments; and sometimes too scrupulous an attention to the style of the structure, occasions a poverty and dulness within, which deprives the buildings of part of their utility. But in a garden they ought to be considered both as beautiful objects, and as agreable retreats; if a character becomes them, it is that of the scene they belong to, not that of their primitive application: a Grecian temple, or Gothic church, may adorn spots where it would be affectation to preserve that solemnity within, which is proper for places of devotion; they are not to be exact models, subjects only of curiosity or study; they are also seats; and such seats will be little frequented by the proprietor; his mind must generally be indisposed to so much simplicity, and so much gloom, in the midst of gaiety, richness, and variety.

But though the interior of buildings should not be disregarded, it is by their exterior that they become *objects*; and sometimes by the one, sometimes by the other, and sometimes by both, they are intitled to be considered as *characters*.


## XL.

As objects, they are designed either to *distinguish*, or to *break*, or to *adorn*, the scenes to which they are applied.

The difference between one wood, one lawn, one piece of water, and another, are not always very apparent; the several parts of a garden would, therefore, often seem similar, if they were not distinguished by buildings; but these are so observable, so obvious at a glance, so easily retained in the memory, they mark the spots where they are placed with so much strength, they attract the relation of all around with so much power, that parts thus distinguished can never be confounded together. Yet it by no means follows, that, therefore, every scene must have its edifice: the want of one is sometimes a variety; and other circumstances are often sufficiently characteristic; it is only when these too nearly agree, that we must have recourse to buildings for differences; we can introduce, exhibit, or contrast them as we please; the most striking object is thereby made a mark of distinction; and the force of this first impression prevents our observing the points of resemblance.

The uniformity of a view may be broken by similar means, and on the same principle: when a wide heath, a dreary moor, or a continued plain is in prospect, objects which catch the eye supply the want of variety; none are so effectual for this purpose as buildings. Plantations or water can have no very sensible effect, unless they are large or numerous, and almost change the character of the scene; but a small single building diverts the attention at once from the sameness of the extent; which it breaks, but does not divide; and diversifies, without altering its nature. The design, however, must not be apparent; the merit of a cottage applied to this purpose, consists in its being free from the suspicion; and a few trees near it will both enlarge the object, and account for its position. Ruins are a hackneyed device immediately detected, unless their style be singular, or their dimensions extraordinary. The semblance of an ancient British monument might be adapted to the same end, with little trouble, and great success; the materials might be brick, or even timber plaistered over, if stone could not easily be procured: whatever they were, the fallacy would not be discernible; it is an object to be seen at a distance, rude and large, and in character agreable to a wild open view: but no building ought to be introduced, which may not in reality belong to such a situation; no Grecian temples, no Turkish mosques, no Egyptian obelisks or pyramids, none imported from foreign countries, and unusual here; the apparent artifice would destroy an effect, which is so nice as to be weakened, if objects proper to produce it are displayed with too much ostentation, if they seem to be contrivances not accidents, and the advantages of their position appear to be more laboured than natural.

But in a garden, where objects are intended only to adorn, every species of architecture may be admitted, from the Grecian down to the Chinese; and the choice is so free, that the mischief most to be apprehended, is an abuse of this latitude in the multiplicity of buildings. Few scenes can bear more than two or three; in some a single one has a greater effect than any number; and a careless glimpse here and there, of such as belong immediately to different parts, frequently enliven the landskip with more spirit that those which are industriously shewn. If the effect of a partial sight, or a distant view, were more attended to, many scenes might be filled, without being crouded; a greater number of buildings would be tolerated, when they seemed to be casual, not forced; and the animation, and the richness of objects, might be had without pretence or display.

Too fond an ostentation of buildings, even of those which are principal, is a common error; and when all is done, they are not always shewn to the greatest advantage. Though their symmetry and their beauties ought in general to be distinctly and fully seen, yet an oblique is sometimes better than a direct view; and they are often less agreable objects when entire, than when a part is covered, or their extent is interrupted; when they are bosomed in wood, as well as backed by it; or appear between the stems of trees which rise before them or above them: thus thrown into perspective, thus grouped and accompanied, they may be as important as if they were quite exposed, and are frequently more picturesque and beautiful.

But a still greater advantage arises from this management, in connecting them with the scene; they are considerable, and different from all around them; inclined therefore to separate from the rest; and yet they are sometimes still more detached by the pains taken to exhibit them: that very importance which is the cause of the distinction, ought to be a reason for guarding against the independence to which it is naturally prone, and by which an object, which ought to be a part of the whole, is reduced to a mere individual. An elevated is generally a noble situation; when it is a point, or a pinnacle, the structure may be a continuation of the ascent; and on many occasions, some parts of the building may descend lower than others, and multiply the appearances of connection; but an edifice in the midst of an extended ridge, commonly seems naked, alone, and imposed upon the brow, not joined to it. If wood to accompany it will not grow there, it had better be brought a little way down the declivity, and then all behind, above, and about it, are so many points of contact, which is incorporated into the landskip.

Accompaniments are important to a building; but they lose much of their effect, when they do not appear to be casual. A little mount just large enough for it; a small piece of water below, of no other use than to reflect it; and a plantation close behind, evidently placed there only to give it relief, are as artificial as the structure itself, and alienate it from the scene of nature into which it is introduced, and to which it ought to be reconciled. These appendages therefore should be so disposed, and so connected with the adjacent parts, as to answer other purposes, though applicable to this, that they may be bonds of union, not marks of difference; and that the situation may appear to have been chosen, at the most, not made for the building.

In the choice of a situation, that which shews the building best, ought generally to be preferred: eminence, relief, and every other advantage which can be, ought to be given to an object of so much consideration: they are for the most part desireable, sometimes necessary, and exceptionable only when, instead of rising out of the scene, they are forced into it; and a contrivance to procure them at any rate, is avowed without any disguise. There are, however, occasions, in which the most tempting advantages of situation must be waved; the general composition may forbid a building in one spot, or require it in another; at other times the interest of the particular groupe it belongs to, may exact a sacrifice of the opportunities to exhibit its beauties and importance; and at all times the pretensions of every individual object must give way to the greater effect of the whole.

## XLI.

The same structure which adorns as an object, may also be expressive as a character; where the former is not wanted, the latter may be desireable; or it may be weak for one purpose, and strong for the other; it may be grave, or gay; magnificent, or simple; and according to its style, may or may not be agreable to the place it is applied to; but mere consistency is not all the merit which buildings can claim: their characters are sometimes strong enough to *determine, improve,* or *correct* that of the scene; and they are so conspicuous, and so distinguished, that whatever force they have is immediately and sensibly felt. They are fit therefore to make a first impression; and when a scene is but faintly characterised, they give at once a cast which spreads over the whole, and which the weaker parts concur to support, though perhaps they were not able to produce it.

Nor do they stop at fixing an uncertainty, or removing a doubt; they raise and enforce a character already marked: a temple adds dignity to the noblest, a cottage simplicity to the most rural scenes; the lightness of a spire, the airiness of an open rotunda, the splendor of a continued colonade, are less ornamental than expressive: others improve chearfulenss into gaiety, gloom into solemnity, and richness into profusion: a retired spot which might have been passed unobserved, is noticed for its tranquility, as soon as it is appropriated by some structure to retreat; and the most unfrequented place seems less solitary than one which appears to have been the haunt of a single individual, or even of a sequestered family, and is marked by a lonely dwelling, or the remains of a deserted habitation.

The means are the same, the application of them only is different, when buildings are used to correct the character of the scene; to enliven its dulness; to mitigate its gloom; or to check its extravagance; and on a variety of occasions to soften, to aggravate, or to counteract, particular circumstances attending it: but care must be taken that they do not contradict too strongly the prevailing idea; they may lessen the dreariness of a waste, but they cannot give it amenity; they may abate horrors, but they will never convert them into graces; they may make a tame scene agreable, and even interesting, not romantic; or turn solemnity into chearfulness, but not into gaiety. In these, and in many other instances, they correct the character, by giving it an inclination towards a better, which is not very different; but they can hardly alter it entirely; when they are totally inconsistent with it, they are at the best nugatory.

The great effects which have been ascribed to buildings, do not depend upon those trivial ornaments, and appendages, which are often too much relied on; such as, the furniture of a hermitage; painted glass in a Gothic church; and sculpture about a Grecian temple; grotesque or bacchanalian figures to denote gaiety; and deaths heads to signify melancholy. Such devices are only descriptive, not expressive, of character; and must not be substituted in the stead of those superior properties, the want of which they acknowledge, but do not supply: they besides often require time to trace their meaning, and to see their application; but the peculiar excellence of buildings is, that their effects are instantaneous, and therefore the impressions they make are forcible: in order to produce such effects, the general style of the structure, and its position, are the principal considerations; either of them will sometimes be strongly characteristic alone: united, their powers are very great; and both are so important, that if they do not concur, at least they must not contradict one another: the colour also of the buildings is seldom a matter of indifference; that excessive brightness which is too indiscriminately used to render them conspicuous, is apt to disturb the harmony of the whole; sometimes makes them too glaring as objects; and is often inconsistent with their characters. When these effectual points are secured, subordinate circumstances may be made to agree with them; and though minute, they may not be improper, if they are not affected; they frequently mark a correspondence between the outside, and the inside of a building; in the latter they are not inconsiderable; they may there be observed at leisure; and there they explain in detail the character which is more generally expressed in the air of the whole.

## XLII.

To enumerate the several buildings which may be used for convenience, or distinction, as ornaments, or as characters, would lead me far from my subject into a treatise of architecture; for every branch of architecture furnishes, on different occasions, objects proper for a garden; and different species may meet in the same composition; no analogy exists between the age and the country, whence they are borrowed, and the spot they are applied to, except in some particular instances; but in general, they are naturalized to a place of the most improved cultivated nature by their effects; beauty is their use; and they are consistent with each other, if all are conformable to the style of the scene, proportioned to its extent, and agreable to its character. On the other hand, varieties more than sufficient for any particular spot, enough for a very extensive view, may be found in every species; to each also belong a number of characters: the Grecian architecture can lay aside its dignity in a rustic building; and the caprice of the Gothic is sometimes not incompatible with greatness; our choice therefore may be confined to the variations of one species, or range through the contrasts of many, as circumstances, taste, or other considerations shall determine.

The choice of situations is also very free; circumstances which are requisite to particular structures, may often be combined happily with others, and enter into a variety of compositions; even where they are appropriated, they may still be applied in several degrees, and the same edifice may thereby be accommodated to very different scenes: some buildings which have a just expression when accompanied with proper appendages, have none without them; they may therefore be characters in one place, and only objects in another. On all these occasions, the application is allowable, if it can be made without inconsistency; a hermitage must not be close to a road, but whether it be exposed to view on the side of a mountain, or concealed in the depth of a wood, is almost a matter of indifference, that it is at a distance from public resort is sufficient: a castle must not be sunk in a bottom; but that it should stand in the utmost pinnacle of a hill, is not necessary; on a lower knole, and backed by the rise, it may appear to greater advantage as an object; and be much more important to the general composition: a tower,

> Bosomed high in tufted trees,

has been selected by one of our greatest poets as a singular beauty; and the justness of his choice has been so generally acknowledged, that the description is become almost proverbial; and yet a tower does not seem designed to be surrounded by a wood; but the appearance may be accounted for; it does sometimes occur; and we are easily satisfied of the propriety, when the effect is so pleasing. Many buildings, which from their splendor best become an open exposure, will yet be sometimes not ill bestowed on a more sequestered spot, either to characterise or adorn it; and others, for which a solitary would in general be preferred to an eminent situation, may occasionally be objects in very conspicuous positions. A Grecian temple, from its peculiar grace and dignity, deserves every distinction; it may, however, in the depth of a wood, be so circumstanced, that the want of those advantages to which it seems entitled, will not be regretted. A happier situation cannot be devised, than that of the temple of Pan, at the *south lodge on Enfield chace. It is of the usual oblong form, encompassed by a colonade; in dimensions, and in style, it is equal to a most extensive landskip; and yet by the antique and rustic air of its Doric columns without bases; by the chastity of its little ornament, a crook, a pipe, and a scrip, and those only over the doors; and by the

---

* A villa belonging to Mr. Sharpe, near Barnet, in Middlesex.

simplicity of the whole, both within and without, it is adapted with so much propriety to the thickets which conceal it from the view, that no one can wish it to be brought forward, who is sensible to the charms of the Arcadian scene which this building alone has created. On the other hand, a very spacious field, or sheep-walk, will not be disgraced by a cottage, a Dutch barn, or a hay-stack; nor will they, though small and familiar, appear to be inconsiderable or insignificant objects. Numberless other instances might be adduced to prove the impossibility of restraining particular buildings to particular situations, upon any general principles; the variety in their forms is hardly greater than in their application.

## XLIII.

To this great variety must be added the many changes which may be made by the means of *ruins*; they are a class by themselves, beautiful as objects, expressive as characters, and peculiarly calculated to connect with their appendages into elegant groupes; they may be accommodated with ease to irregularity of ground, and their disorder is improved by it; they may be intimately blended with trees and with thickets, and the interruption is an advantage; for imperfection and obscurity are their properties; and to carry the imagination to something greater than is seen, their effect. They may for any of these purposes be separated into detached pieces; contiguity is not necessary, nor even the appearance of it, if the relation be preserved; but straggling ruins have a bad effect, when the several parts are equally considerable. There should be one large mass to raise an idea of greatness, to attract the others about it, and to be a common centre of union to all: the smaller pieces then mark the original dimensions of one extensive structure; and no longer appear to be the remains of several little buildings.

All remains excite an enquiry into the former state of the edifice, and fix the mind in a contemplation of the use it was applied to; besides the characters expressed by their style and position, they suggest ideas which would not arise from the buildings, if entire. The purposes of many have ceased; an abbey, or a castle, if complete, can now be no more than a dwelling; the memory of the times, and of the manners, to which they were adapted, is preserved only in history, and in ruins; and certain sensations of regret, of veneration, or compassion, attend the recollection: nor are these confined to the remains of buildings which are now in disuse; those of an old mansion raise reflections on the domestic comforts once enjoyed, and the antient hospitality which reigned there. Whatever building we see in decay, we naturally contrast its present to its former state, and delight to ruminate on the comparison. It is true that such effects properly belong to real ruins; they are however produced in a certain degree by those which are fictitious; the impressions are not so strong, but they are exactly similar; and the representation, though it does not present facts to the memory, yet suggests subjects to the imagination: but, in order to affect the fancy, the supposed original design should be clear, the use obvious, and the form easy to be traced; no fragments should be hazarded without a precise meaning, and an evident connection; none should be perplexed in their construction, or uncertain as to their application. Conjectures about the form, raise doubts about the existence of the ancient structure; the mind must not be allowed to hesitate; it must be hurried away from examining into the reality, by the exactness and the force of the resemblance.

In the ruins of * Tintern abbey, the original construction of the church is perfectly marked; and it is principally from this circumstance that they are celebrated as a subject of curiosity

* Between Chepstowe and Monmouth.

and contemplation. The walls are almost entire; the roof only is fallen in; but most of the columns which divided the isles are still standing; of those which have dropped down, the bases remain, every one exactly in its place; and in the middle of the nave four lofty arches, which once supported the steeple, rise high in the air above all the rest, each reduced now to a narrow rim of stone, but completely preserving its form. The shapes even of the windows are little altered; but some of them are quite obscured, others partially shaded, by tufts of ivy, and those which are most clear, are edged with its slender tendrils, and lighter foliage, wreathing about the sides and the divisions; it winds round the pillars; it clings to the walls; and in one of the isles, clusters at the top in bunches so thick and so large, as to darken the space below. The other isles, and the great nave, are exposed to the sky; the floor is entirely overspread with turf; and to keep it clean from weeds and bushes, is now its highest preservation. Monkish tomb-stones, and the monuments of benefactors long since forgotten, appear above the greenswerd; the bases of the pillars which have fallen, rise out of it; and maimed effigies, and sculpture worn with age and weather, Gothic capitals, carved cornices, and various fragments, are scattered about, or lie in heaps piled up together. Other shattered pieces, though disjointed and mouldering, still occupy their original places; and a stair-case much impaired, which led to a tower now no more, is suspended at a great height, uncovered and inaccessible. Nothing is perfect; but memorials of every part still subsist; all certain, but all in decay; and suggesting, at once, every idea which can occur in a seat of devotion, solitude, and desolation. Upon such models, fictitious ruins should be formed; and if any parts are entirely lost, they should be such as the imagination can easily supply from those which are still remaining. Distinct traces of the building which is supposed to have existed, are less liable to the suspicion of artifice, than an unmeaning heap of confusion. Precision is always satisfactory; but in the reality it is only agreable; in the copy, it is essential to the imitation.

A material circumstance to the truth of the imitation, is, that the ruin appear to be very old; the idea is besides interesting in itself; a monument of antiquity is never seen with indifference; and a semblance of age may be given to the representation, by the hue of the materials; the growth of ivy, and other plants; and cracks and fragments seemingly occasioned rather by decay, than by destruction. An appendage evidently more modern than the principal structure will sometimes corroborate the effect; the shed of a cottager amidst the remains of a temple, is a contrast both to the former and the present state of the building; and a tree flourishing among ruins, shews the length of time they have lain neglected. No circumstance so forcibly marks the desolation of a spot once inhabited, as the prevalence of nature over it:

> Campos ubi Troja fuit

is a sentence which conveys a stronger idea of a city totally overthrown, than a description of its remains; but in a representation to the eye, some remains must appear; and then the perversion of them to an ordinary use, or an intermixture of a vigorous vegetation, intimates a settled despair of their restoration.

## Of ART.

### XLIV.

The several constituent parts of the scenes of nature having now been considered, the next enquiry is into the particular principles and circumstances which may affect them, when they are applied to the subjects of gardening. It has always been supposed, that *art* must then interfere; but art was carried to excess, when from accessory it became principal; and the subject upon which it was employed, was brought under regulations, less applicable to that than to any other; when ground, wood, and water, were reduced to mathematical figures; and similarity and order were preferred to freedom and variety. These mischiefs, however, were occasioned, not by the use, but the perversion of art; it excluded, instead of improving upon nature; and thereby destroyed the very end it was called in to promote.

So strange an abuse probably arose from an idea of some necessary correspondence between the mansion, and the scene it immediately commanded; the forms, therefore, of both were determined by the same rules; and terraces, canals, and avenues, were but so many variations of the plan of the building. The regularity thus established spread afterwards to more distant quarters: there, indeed, the absurdity was acknowledged as soon as a more natural disposition appeared; but a prejudice in favour of art, as it is called, *just about the house*, still remains. If by the term, *regularity* is intended, the principle is equally applicable to the vicinity of any other building; and every temple in the garden ought to have its concomitant formal slopes and plantations; or the conformity may be reversed, and we may as reasonably contend that the building ought to be irregular, in order to be consistent with the scene it belongs to. The truth is, that both propositions are erroneous; architecture requires symmetry; the objects of nature freedom; and the properties of the one, cannot with justice be transferred to the other. But if by the term, no more is meant than merely *design*, the dispute is at an end; choice, arrangement, composition, improvement, and preservation, are so many symptoms of art, which may occasionally appear in several parts of a garden, but ought to be displayed without reserve near the house; nothing there should seem neglected; it is a scene of the most cultivated nature; it ought to be enriched; it ought to be adorned; and design may be avowed in the plan, and expence in the execution.

Even regularity is not excluded: so capital a structure may extend its influence beyond its walls; but this power should be exercised only over its immediate appendages; the platform upon which the house stands, is generally continued to a certain breadth on every side; and whether it be pavement or gravel, may undoubtedly coincide with the shape of the building. The road which leads up to the door may go off from it in an equal angle, so that the two sides shall exactly correspond: and certain ornaments, though detached, are yet rather within the province of architecture than of gardening; works of sculpture are not, like buildings, objects familiar in scenes of cultivated nature; but vases, statues, and termini, are usual appendages to a considerable edifice; as such they may attend the mansion, and trespass a little upon the garden, provided they are not carried so far into it as to lose their connection with the structure. The platform and the road are also appurtenances to the house; all these may therefore be adapted to its form; and the environs will thereby acquire a degree of regularity; but to give it to the objects of nature, only on account of their proximity to others which are calculated to receive it, is, at the best, a refinement.

## XLV.

Upon the same principles regularity has been required in the *approach*; and an additional reason has been assigned for it, that the idea of a seat is thereby extended to a distance; but that may be done by other means than by an avenue; a private road is easily known; if carried through grounds, or a park, it is commonly very apparent; even in a lane, here and there a bench, a painted gate, a small plantation, or any other little ornament, will sufficiently denote it; if the entrance only be marked, simple preservation will retain the impression along the whole progress; or the road may wind through several scenes distinguished by objects, or by an extraordinary degree of cultivation; and then the length of the way, and the variety of improvements through which it is conducted, may extend the appearance of domain, and the idea of a seat, beyond the reach of any direct avenue.

An avenue being confined to one termination, and excluding every view on the sides, has a tedious sameness throughout; to be great, it must be dull; and the object to which it is appropriated, is after all seldom shewn to advantage. Buildings, in general, do not appear so large, and are not so beautiful, when looked at in front, as when they are seen from an angular station, which commands two sides at once, and throws them both into perspective: but a winding lateral approach is free from these objections; it may besides be brought up to the house without disturbing any of the views from it; but an avenue cuts the scenery directly in two, and reduces all the prospect to a narrow vista. A mere line of perspective, be the extent what it may, will seldom compensate for the loss of that space which it divides, and of the parts which it conceals.

The approach to * Caversham, though a mile in length, and not once in sight of the house, till close upon it, yet can never be mistaken for any other way than it is; a passage only through a park is not introduced with so much distinction, so precisely marked, or kept in such preservation. On each side of the entrance is an elegant lodge; the interval between them is a light open pallisade, crossing the whole breadth of a lovely valley; the road is conducted along the bottom, continually winding in natural easy sweeps, and presenting at every bend some new scene to the view; at last it gently slants up the side of a little rise to the mansion, where the eminence, which seemed inconsiderable, is found to be a very elevated situation, to which the approach, without once quitting the valley, had been insensibly ascending, all the way. In its progress, it never breaks the

---

* The seat of lord Cadogan, near Reading.

scenes through which it passes; the plantations and the glades are continued without interruption, quite across the valley; the opposite sides have a relation to each other, not answering, not contrasted, but connected; nor does the disposition ever seem to have been made with any attention to the road; but the scenes still belong purely to the park; each of them is preserved entire; and avails itself of all the space which the situation will allow. At the entrance the slopes are very gentle, with a few large hawthorns, beeches, and oaks, scattered over them; these are thickened by the perspective as the valley winds; and just at the bend, a large clump hangs on a bold ascent, from whence different groupes, growing gradually less and less till they end in single trees, stretch quite away to a fine grove which crowns the opposite brow: the road passes between the groupes, under a light and lofty arch of ash; and then opens upon a glade, broken on the left only by a single tree; and on the right by several beeches standing so close together as to be but one in appearance: this glade is bounded by a beautiful grove, which in one part spreads a perfect gloom, but in others divides into different clusters, which leave openings for the gleams of light to pour in between them. It extends to the edge, and borders for some way the side, of a collateral dale, which retires slowly from the view; and in which the falls of the ground are more tame, the bottom more flattened, than in the principal valley; the banks of this also near the junction, are more gentle than before; but on the opposite side, the steeps and the clumps still continue; and amongst them is a fine knole, from which descend two or three groupes of large trees, feathering down to the bottom, and by the pendency of their branches favouring the declivity. To these succeeds an open space, diversified only by a few scattered trees; and in the midst of it, some magnificent beeches crouding together, overshadow the road, which is carried through a narrow, darksome passage between them: soon after it rises under a thick wood in the garden up to the house, where it suddenly bursts out upon a rich, and extensive prospect, with the town and the churches of Reading in full sight, and the hills of Windsor forest in the horizon. Such a view at the end of a long avenue, would have been, at the best, but a compensation for the tediousness of the way; but here the approach is as delightful as the termination: yet even in this, a similarity of style may be said to prevail; but it has every variety of open plantations; and these are not confusedly thrown together, but formed into several scenes, all of them particularly marked: one is characterised by a grove; the next by clumps; and others by little groupes, or single trees: the plantations sometimes cover only the brow, and retire along the top from the view; sometimes they seem to be suspended on the edge, or the sides of the descents; in one place they leave the bottom clear; in another they overspread the whole valley: the intervals are often little less than lawns; at other times they are no more than narrow glades between the groves; or only small openings in the midst of a plantation. The ground, without being broken into diminutive parts, is cast into an infinite number of elegant shapes, in every gradation from the most gentle slope, to a very precipitate fall: the trees also are of several kinds, and their shadows of various tints; those of the horse-chesnuts are dark; the beeches spread a broader but less gloomy obscurity; and they are often so vast, they swell out in a succession of such enormous masses, that, though contiguous, a deep shade sinks in between them, and distinguishes each immense individual: such intervals are in some places filled up with other species; the maples are of so extraordinary a size, that they do not appear inconsiderable, when close to the forest trees; large hawthorns, some oaks, and in one part many, perhaps too many limes, the remains of former avenues, are intermixed; and amongst all these often rise the tallest ash, whose lighter foliage only chequers the turf beneath, while their peculiar hue diversifies the greens of the groupes they belong to. After enumerating the beauties of this approach, and reflecting that they are confined within a narrow valley, without views, buildings or water, another can hardly be conceived so destitute of the means of variety, as to justify the sameness of an avenue.


## XLVI.

If regularity is not entitled to a preference in the environs or approach to a house, it will be difficult to support its pretensions to a place, in any more *distant parts* of a park or a garden. Formal slopes of ground are ugly; right or circular lines bounding water, do not indeed change the nature of the element; it still retains some of its agreable properties; but the shape given to it is disgusting. Regularity in plantations is less offensive; we are habituated, as has been already observed, to straight lines of trees, in cultivated nature; a double row, meeting at the top, and forming a complete arched vista, has a peculiar effect; other regular figures have a degree of beauty; and to alter or to disguise such a disposition, without destroying a number of fine trees, which cannot well be spared, may sometimes be difficult; but it hardly ever ought to be chosen in the arrangement of a young plantation.

Regularity was, however, once thought essential to every garden, and every approach; and it yet remains in many. It is still a character, denoting the neighbourhood of a gentleman's habitation; and an avenue, as an object in a view, gives to a house, otherwise inconsiderable, the air of a mansion. Buildings which answer one another at the entrance of an approach, or on the sides of an opening, have a similar effect; they distinguish at once the precincts of a seat from the rest of the country. Some pieces of sculpture also, such as vases and termini, may perhaps now and then be used, to extend the appearance of a garden beyond its limits, and to raise the mead in which they are placed above the ordinary improvements of cultivated nature.

At other times they may be applied as ornaments to the most polished lawns; the traditional ideas we have conceived of Arcadian scenes, correspond with such decorations; and sometime a solitary urn, inscribed to the memory of a person now no more, but who once frequented the shades where it stands, is an object equally elegant and interesting. The occasions, however, on which we may, with any propriety, trespass beyond the bounds of cultivated nature, are very rare; the force of the character can alone excuse the artifice avowed in expressing it.

## Of PICTURESQUE BEAUTY.

### XLVII.

But regularity can never attain to a great share of beauty, and to none of the species called *picturesque*; a denomination in general expressive of excellence, but which, by being too indiscriminately applied, may be sometimes productive of errors. That a subject is recommended at least to our notice, and probably to our favour, if it has been distinguished by the pencil of an eminent painter, is indisputable; we are delighted to see those objects in the reality, which we are used to admire in the representation; and we improve upon their intrinsic merit, by recollecting their effects in the picture. The greatest beauties of nature will often suggest the remembrance; for it is the business of a landskip painter to select them; and his choice is absolutely unrestrained; he is at liberty to exclude all objects which may hurt the composition; he has the power of combining those which he admits in the most agreable manner; he can even determine the season of the year, and the hour of the day, to shew his landskip in whatever light he prefers. The works therefore of a great master, are fine exhibitions of nature, and an excellent school wherein to form a taste for beauty; but still their authority is not absolute;

they must be used only as studies, not as models; for a picture and a scene in nature, though they agree in many, yet differ in some particulars, which must always be taken into consideration, before we can decide upon the circumstances which may be transferred from the one to the other.

In their *dimensions* the distinction is obvious; the same objects on different scales have very different effects; those which seem monstrous on the one, may appear diminutive on the other; and a form, which is elegant in a small object, may be too delicate for a large one. Besides, in a canvas of a few feet, there is not room for every species of variety which in nature is pleasing. Though the characteristic distinction of trees may be marked, their more minute differences, which however enrich plantations, cannot be expressed; and a multiplicity of enclosures, catches of water, cottages, cattle and a thousand other circumstances, which enliven a prospect, are, when reduced into a narrow compass, no better than a heap of confusion. Yet, on the other hand, the principal objects must often be more diversified in a picture than in a scene; a building which occupies a considerable portion of the former, will appear small in the latter, when compared to the space all around it; and the number of parts which may be necessary to break its sameness in the one, will aggravate its insignificance in the other. A tree which presents one rich mass of foliage, has sometimes a fine effect in nature; but when painted, is often a heavy lump, which can be lightened only by separating the boughs, and shewing the ramifications between them. In several other instances the object is frequently affected by the proportion it bears to the actual, not the ideal, circumjacent extent.

Painting, with all its powers, is still more unequal to some subjects, and can give only *a faint, if any, representation* of them; but a gardener is not therefore to reject them; he is not debarred from a view down the sides of a hill, or a prospect where the horizon is lower than the station, because he never saw them in a picture. Even when painting exactly imitates the appearances of nature, it is often weak in conveying the *ideas* which they excite, and on which much of their effect sometimes depends. This however is not always a disadvantage; the appearance may be more pleasing than the idea which accompanies it; and the omission of the one may be an improvement of the other; many beautiful tints denote disagreeable circumstances; the hue of a barren heath is often finely diversified; a piece of bare ground is sometimes overspread with a number of delicate shades; and yet we prefer a more uniform verdure to all their variety. In a picture, the several tints which occur in nature may be blended, and retain only their beauty, without suggesting the poverty of the soil which occasions them; but in the reality, the cause is more powerful than the effect; we are less pleased with the sight, than we are hurt by the reflection; and a most agreeable mixture of colours may present no other idea than of dreariness and sterility.

On the other hand, *utility* will sometimes supply the want of beauty in the reality, but not in a picture. In the former, we are never totally inattentive to it; we are familiarised to the marks of it; and we allow a degree of merit to an object which has no other recommendation. A regular building is generally more agreeable in a scene than in a picture; and an adjacent platform, if evidently convenient, is tolerable in the one; it is always a right line too much in the other. Utility is at the least an excuse, when it is real; but it is an idea never included in the representation.

Many more instances might be alleged to prove, that the subjects for a painter and a gardener are not always the same; some which are agreeable in the reality, lose their effect in the imitation; and others, at the best, have less merit in a scene than in a picture. The term picturesque is therefore applicable only to such objects in nature, as, after allowing for the differences between the arts of painting and of gardening, are fit to be formed into groupes, or to enter into a composition, where the several parts have a relation to each other; and in opposition to those which may be spread abroad in detail, and have no merit but as individuals.

## Of CHARACTER.

### XLVIII.

Character is very reconcileable with beauty; and even when independent of it, has attracted so much regard, as to occasion several frivolous attempts to produce it; statues, inscriptions, and even paintings, history and mythology, and a variety of devices have been introduced for this purpose. The heathen deities and heroes have therefore had their several places assigned to them in the woods and the lawns of a garden; natural cascades have been disfigured with river gods; and columns erected only to receive quotations; the compartments of a summer-house have been filled with pictures of gambols and revels, as significant of gaiety; the cypress, because it was once used in funerals, has been thought peculiarly adapted to melancholy; and the decorations, the furniture, and the environs of a building have been crouded with puerilities, under pretence of propriety. All these devices are rather *emblematical* than expressive; they may be ingenious contrivances, and recall absent ideas to the recollection; but they make no immediate impression; for they must be examined, compared, perhaps explained, before the whole design of them is well understood: and though an allusion to a favourite or well-known subject of history, of poetry, or of tradition, may now and then animate or dignify a scene, yet as the subject does not naturally belong to a garden, the allusion should not be principal; it should seem to have been suggested by the scene;

a transitory image, which irresistibly occurred; not sought for, not laboured; and have the force of a metaphor, free from the detail of an allegory.

## XLIX.

Another species of character arises from direct *imitation*; when a scene or an object, which has been celebrated in description, or is familiar in idea, is represented in a garden. Artificial ruins, lakes, and rivers, fall under this denomination; the air of a seat extended to a distance, and scenes calculated to raise ideas of Arcadian elegance, or of rural simplicity, with many more which have been occasionally mentioned, or will obviously occur, may be ranked in this class; they are all representations; but the materials, the dimensions, and other circumstances, being the same in the copy and the original, their effects are similar in both; and if not equally strong, the defect is not in the resemblance; but the consciousness of an imitation, checks that train of thought which the appearance naturally suggests; yet an over-anxious sollicitude to disguise the fallacy is often the means of exposing it; too many points of likeness sometimes hurt the deception; they seem studied and forced; and the affectation of resemblance destroys the supposition of a reality. A hermitage is the habitation of a recluse; it should be distinguished by its solitude, and its simplicity; but if it is filled with crucifixes, hour-glasses, beads, and every other trinket which can be thought of, the attention is diverted from enjoying the retreat to examining the particulars; all the collateral circumstances which agree with a character, seldom meet in one subject; and when they are industriously brought together, though each be natural, the collection is artificial.

The peculiar advantages which gardening has over other imitative arts, will not, however, support attempts to introduce, they rather forbid the introduction of characters, to which the space is not adequate. A plain simple field, unadorned but with the common rural appendages, is an agreable opening; but if it is extremely small, neither a hay-stack, nor a cottage, nor a stile, nor a path, nor much less all of them together, will give it an air of reality. A harbour or an artificial lake is but a conceit: it raises no idea of refuge or security; for the lake does not suggest an idea of danger; it is detached from the large body of water; and yet it is in itself but a poor inconsiderable basin, vainly affecting to mimick the majesty of the sea. When imitative characters in gardening are egregiously defective in any material circumstance, the truth of the others exposes and aggravates the failure.

## L.

But the art of gardening aspires to more than imitation: it can create *original* characters, and give expressions to the several scenes superior to any they can receive from allusions. Certain properties, and certain dispositions, of the objects of nature, are adapted to excite particular ideas and sensations: many of them have been occasionally mentioned; and all are very well known: they require no discernment, examination, or discussion, but are obvious at a glance, and instantaneously distinguished by our feelings. Beauty alone is not so engaging as this species of character; the impressions it makes are more transient and less interesting; for it aims only at delighting the eye, but the other affects our sensibility. An assemblage of the most elegant forms in the happiest situations is to a degree indiscriminate, if they have not been selected and arranged with a design to produce certain expressions; an air of magnificence, or of simplicity, of chearfulness, tranquility, or some other general character, ought to pervade the whole; and objects pleasing in themselves, if they contradict that character, should therefore be excluded; those which are only indifferent must sometimes make room for such as are more significant; many will often be introduced for no other merit than their expression; and some which are in general rather disagreable, may occasionally be recommended by it. Barrenness itself may be an acceptable circumstance in a spot dedicated to solitude and melancholy.

The power of such characters is not confined to the ideas which the objects immediately suggest; for these are connected with others, which insensibly lead to subjects, far distant perhaps from the original thought, and related to it only by a similitude in the sensations they excite. In a prospect, enriched and enlivened with inhabitants and cultivation, the attention is caught at first by the circumstances which are gayest in their season, the bloom of an orchard, the festivity of a hay-field, and the carols of harvest-home; but the chearfulness which these infuse into the mind, expands afterwards to other objects than those immediately presented to the eye; and we are thereby disposed to receive, and delighted to pursue, a variety of pleasing ideas, and every benevolent feeling. At the sight of a ruin, reflections on the change, the decay, and the desolation before us, naturally occur; and they introduce a long succession of others, all tinctured with that melancholy which these have inspired: or if the monument revive the memory of former times, we do not stop at the simple fact which it records, but recollect many more coaeval circumstances, which we see, not perhaps as they were, but as they are come down to us, venerable with age, and magnified by fame; even without the assistance of buildings, or other adventitious circumstances, nature alone furnishes materials for scenes, which may be adapted to almost every kind of expression; their operation is general; and their consequences infinite: the mind is elevated, depressed or composed, as gaiety, gloom, or tranquility, prevail in the scene; and we soon lose sight of the means by which the character is formed; we forget the particular objects it presents; and giving way to their effects, without recurring to the cause, we follow the track they have begun, to any extent, which the disposition they accord with will allow: it suffices that the scenes of nature have a power to affect our imagination and our sensibility; for such is the constitution of the human mind, that if once it is agitated, the emotion often spreads far beyond the occasion; when the passions are roused, their course is unrestrained; when the fancy is on the wing, its flight is unbounded; and quitting the inanimate objects which first gave them their spring, we may be led by thought above thought, widely differing in degree, but still corresponding in character, till we rise from familiar subjects up to the sublimest conceptions, and are rapt in the contemplation of whatever is great or beautiful, which we see in nature, feel in man, or attribute to divinity.

## Of the GENERAL SUBJECT.

### LI.

The scenes of nature are also affected by the general subject to which they are applied, whether that be a *farm*, a *garden*, a *park*, or a *riding*. These may all indeed be parts of one place; they may border on each other; they may to a degree be intermixed; but each is still a character of such force, that whichever prevails, the propriety of all other characters, and of every species of beauty, must be tried by their conformity to this: and circumstances necessary to one, may be inconsistencies in the rest; *elegance* is the peculiar excellence of a garden; *greatness* of a park; *simplicity* of a farm; and *pleasantness* of a riding. These distinguishing properties will alone exclude from the one, many objects which are very acceptable in the others; but these are not the only properties in which they essentially differ.

A garden is intended to walk or to sit in, which are circumstances not considered in a riding; a park comprehends all the use of the other two; and these uses determine the *proportional extent* of each; a large garden would be but a small park; and the circumference of a considerable park but a short riding. A farm is in some measure denominated from its size; if it greatly exceed the dimensions of a garden, so that its bounds are beyond the reach of a walk, it becomes a riding. A farm and a garden hence appear to be calculated for indolent, a riding for active amusements; and a park for both; seats, therefore, and buildings for refreshment or indulgence, should be frequent in a garden or a farm; should sometimes occur in a park, but are unnecessary in a riding.

Within the narrow compass of a garden, there is not room for *distant effects*; on the other hand, it allows of objects which are striking only in a *single point of view*; for we may stop there to contemplate them; and an obscure catch, or a partial glimpse of others, are also acceptable circumstances, in the leisure of a seat, or even in the course of a loitering walk. But these are lost in a riding, where the pleasantness of the road, not of the spot, is the principal consideration; and its greatest improvement is a distant object, which may be seen from several points, or along a considerable part of the way. *Minute beauties* in general may abound in a garden: they may be frequent in a farm; in both we have opportunities to observe, and to examine them; in a park they are below our notice; in a riding they escape it.

*Prospects* are agreeable to either of the four general subjects; but not equally necessary to all. In a garden, or in a farm, scenes within themselves are often satisfactory; and in their retired spots an opening would be improper. A park is defective, if confined to its inclosure; a perpetual succession of home scenes, through so large an extent, wants variety; and fine prospects are circumstances of greatness; but they are not required in every part; the place itself supplies many noble views; and these are not much improved by a distant rim, or a little peep of the country, which is inadequate to the rest of the composition. A riding has seldom much beauty of its own; it depends on objects without for its pleasantness; if it only leads now and then to a striking point, and is dull all the rest of the way, it will not be much frequented; but very moderate views are sufficient to render its progress agreable.

By concealing therefore much of the prospects, we destroy the amusement of a riding; the view of the country should not be hurt by the improvements of the road. In a garden, on the contrary, continuation of shade is very acceptable; and if the views be sometimes interrupted, they may still be caught from many points; we may enjoy them there whenever we please; and they would pall if constantly in sight. The best situation for a house is not that which has the greatest command; a chearfull look-out from the windows is all that the proprietor desires; he is more sensible to the charms of the greater prospects, if he sees them only occasionally, and they do not become insipid by being familiar; for the same reason he does not wish for them in every part of his garden; and temporary concealments give them fresh spirit whenever they appear; but the views of a riding are not visited so often, as thereby to lose any of their effect. Plantations therefore in a country should be calculated rather for objects to look at, than for shades to pass through: in a park, they may answer both purposes; but in a garden, they are commonly considered as places to walk or to sit in; as such too they are most welcome in a farm; but still the distinction between an improved and an ordinary farm being by no circumstance so sensibly marked, as by the arrangement of the trees, they are more important as objects there than in a garden.

Though a farm and a garden agree in many particulars connected with extent, yet in *style* they are the two extremes. Both indeed are subjects of cultivation; but cultivation in the one is *husbandry*; and in the other *decoration*: the former is appropriated to *profit*, the latter to *pleasure*: fields profusely ornamented do not retain the appearance of a farm; and an apparent attention to produce, obliterates the idea of a garden. A park is sometimes not much hurt by being turned to account. The use of a riding is to lead from one beauty to another, and be a scene of pleasure all the way. Made avowedly for that purpose only, it admits more embellishment and distinction, than an ordinary road through a farm.

## Of a FARM.

### LII.

In speculation it might have been expected that the first essays of improvement should have been on a *farm*, to make it both advantageous and delightful; but the fact was otherwise; a small plot was appropriated to pleasure; the rest was preserved for profit only; and this may, perhaps, have been a principal cause of the vicious taste which long prevailed in gardens: it was imagined that a spot set apart from the rest should not be like them; the conceit introduced deviations from nature, which were afterwards carried to such an excess, that hardly any objects truly rural were left within the enclosure, and the view of those without was generally excluded. The first step, therefore, towards a reformation, was by opening the garden to the country, and that immediately led to assimilating them; but still the idea of a spot appropriated to pleasure only prevailed; and one of the latest improvements has been to blend the useful with the agreable; even the ornamented farm was prior in time to the more rural; and we have at last returned to simplicity by force of refinement.

The ideas of *pastoral poetry* seem now to be the standard of that simplicity; and a place conformable to them is deemed a farm in its utmost purity. An allusion to them evidently enters into the design of * the Leasowes, where they appear so lovely as to endear the memory of their author; and justify the reputation of Mr. Shenstone, who inhabited, made, and celebrated the place; it is a perfect picture of his mind, simple, elegant, and amiable; and will always suggest a doubt, whether the spot inspired his verse, or whether, in the scenes which he formed, he only realized the pastoral images which abound in his songs. The whole is in the same taste, yet full of variety; and except in two or three trifles, every part is rural and natural. It is literally a grazing farm lying round the house; and a walk as unaffected and as unadorned as a common field path, is conducted through the several enclosures.

Near the entrance into the grounds, this walk plunges suddenly into a dark narrow dell, filled with small trees which grow upon abrupt, and broken steeps, and watered by a brook, which falls among roots and stones down a natural cascade into the hollow. The stream at first is rapid and open; it is afterwards concealed by thickets, and can be traced only by its murmurs; but it is tamer when it appears again; and gliding then between little groupes of trees, loses itself at last in a piece of water just below. The end of this sequestered spot opens to a pretty landskip, which is very simple; for the parts are but few, and all the objects are familiar; they are only the piece of water, some fields on an easy ascent beyond it, and the steeple of a church above them.

The next scene is more solitary: it is confined within itself, a rude neglected bottom, the sides of which are over-run with bushes and fern, interspersed with several trees. A rill runs also through this little valley, issuing from a wood which hangs on one of the declivities; the stream winds through the wood in a

---

* In Shropshire, between Birmingham and Strourbridge. The late Mr. Dodsley published a more particular description than is here given of the Leasowes; and to that the reader is referred for the detail of those scenes of which he will here find only a general idea.

succession of cascades, down a quick descent of an hundred and fifty yards in continuance; alders and hornbeam grow in the midst of its bed; they shoot up in several stems from the same root; and the current trickles amongst them. On the banks are some considerable trees, which spread but a chequered shade, and let in here and there a sun-beam to play upon the water: beyond them is a slight coppice, just sufficient to skreen the spot from open view; but it casts no gloom; and the space within is all an animated scene; the stream has a peculiar vivacity; and the singular appearance of the upper falls, high in the trees, and seen through the boughs, is equally romantic, beautiful, and lively. The walk having passed through this wood, returns into the same valley, but into another part of it, similar in itself to the former; and yet they appear to be very different scenes, from the conduct only of the path; for in the one, it is open, in the bottom, and perfectly retired; in the other, it is on the brow, it is shaded, and it over-looks not only the little wild below, but some cornfields also on the opposite side, which by their chearfulness and their proximity dissipate every idea of solitude.

At the extremity of the vale is a grove of large forest trees, inclining down a steep declivity; and near it are two fields, both irregular, both beautiful, but distinguished in every particular: the variety of the Leasowes is wonderful; all the enclosures are totally different; there is seldom a single circumstance in which they agree. Of these near the grove, the lower field comprehends both the sides of a deep dip: the upper is one large knole; the former is encompassed with thick wood; the latter is open; a slight hedge, and a serpentine river, are all its boundary. Several trees, single or in groupes, are scattered over the swells of the ground: not a tree is to be seen on all the steeps of the hollow. The path creeps under a hedge round the one, and catches here and there only peeps of the country. It runs directly across the other to the highest eminence, and bursts at once upon the view.

This prospect is also a source of endless variety: it is chearful and extensive, over a fine hilly country, richly cultivated, and full of objects and inhabitants: Hales Owen, a large town, is near; and the Wrekin, at thirty miles distance, is distinctly visible in the horizon. From the knole, which has been mentioned, it is seen altogether, and the beautiful farm of the Leasowes is included in the landskip. In other spots, plantations have been raised, or openings cut, on purpose to shut out, or let in, parts of it, at certain points of view. Just below the principal eminence, which commands the whole, is a seat, where all the striking objects being hid by a few trees, the scene is simply a range of enclosed country. This at other seats is excluded, and only the town, or the church, or the steeple without the church, appears. A village, a farm house, or a cottage, which had been unobserved in the confusion of the general prospect, becomes principal in more contracted views; and the same object which at one place seemed exposed and solitary, is accompanied at another with a foreground of wood, or backed by a beautiful hill. The attention to every circumstance which could diversify the scene has been indefatigable; but the art of the contrivance can never be perceived; the effect always seems accidental.

The transitions also are generally very sudden: from this elevated and gay situation, the change is immediate to sober and quiet home views. The first is a pasture, elegant as a polished lawn, in size not diminutive, and enriched with several fine trees scattered over ground which lies delightfully. Just below it is a little waste, shut up by rude steeps, and wild hanging coppices; on one side of which is a wood, full of large timber trees, and thick with underwood. This receives into its bosom a small irregular piece of water, the other end of which is open; and the light there breaking in enlivens all the rest; even where trees over-hang, or thickets border upon the banks, tho' the reflection of the shadows, the stillness of the water, and the depth of the wood, spread a composure over the whole scene; yet the coolness of it strikes no chill; the shade spreads no gloom; the retreat is peaceful and silent, but not solemn; a refreshing shelter from the scorching heat of noon, without suggesting the most distant idea of the damp and the darkness of night.

A rill much more gentle than any of the former, runs from this piece of water, through a coppice of considerable length, dropping here and there down a shallow fall, or winding about little aits, in which some groupes of small trees are growing. The path is conducted along the bank to the foot of a hill, which it climbs in an awkward zig-zag; and on the top it enters a straight walk, over-arched with trees: but though the ascent and the terrace command charming prospects, they are both too artificial for the character of the Leasowes. The path, however, as soon as it is freed from this restraint, recovers its former simplicity; and descends through several fields, from which are many pretty views of the farm, distinguished by the varieties of the ground, the different enclosures, the hedges, the hedge-rows, and the thickets, which divide them; or the clumps, the single trees, and now and then a hay-stack, which sometimes break the lines of the boundaries, and sometimes stand out in the midst of the pastures.

At the end of the descent, an enchanting grove overspreads a small valley, the abrupt sides of which forms the banks of a lovely rivulet, which winds along the bottom: the stream rushes into the dell by a very precipitate cascade, which is seen through openings in the trees, glimmering at a distance among the shades which over-hang it: the current, as it proceeds, drops down several falls; but between them it is placid and smooth; it is every where clear, and sometimes dappled by gleams of light; while the shadow of every single leaf is marked on the water; and the verdure of the foliage, above, of the moss, and the grass, and the wild plants, on the brink, seems brightened in the reflection: various pretty clusters of open coppice wood are dispersed about the banks; stately forest trees rise in beautiful groupes upon fine swelling knoles above them; and often one or two detached from the rest, incline down the slopes, or slant across the stream: as the valley descends it grows more gloomy; the rivulet is lost in a pool, which is dull, encompassed and darkened by large trees; and just before the stream enters it, in the midst of a plantation of yews, is a bridge of one arch, built of a dusky coloured stone, and simple even to rudeness; but this gloom is not a black spot, ill-united with the rest; it is only a deeper cast of shade; no part of the scene is lightsome; a solemnity prevails over the whole; and it receives an additional dignity from an inscription on a small obelisk, dedicating the grove to the genius of Virgil; near to this delightful spot is the first entrance into the grounds; and thither the walk immediately tends, along the side of a rill.

But it would be injustice to quit the Leasowes, without mentioning one or two circumstances, which in following the course of the walk could not well be taken notice of. The art with which the divisions between the fields are diversified is one of them; even the hedges are distinguished from each other; a common quickset fence is in one place the separation; in another, it is a lofty hedge-row, thick from the top to the bottom; in a third it is a continued range of trees, with all their stems clear, and the light appearing in the intervals between their boughs, and the bushes beneath them; in others these lines of trees are broken, a few groupes only being left at different distances; and sometimes a wood, a grove, a coppice, or a thicket, is the apparent boundary, and by them both the shape, and the style of the enclosures are varied.

The inscriptions which abound in the place, are another striking peculiarity; they are well known and justly admired; and the elegance of the poetry, and the aptness of the quotations, atone for their length and their number; but in general, inscriptions please no more than once; the utmost they can pretend to, except when their allusions are emblematical, is to point out the beauties, or describe the effects, of the spots they belong to; but those beauties and those effects must be very faint, which stand in need of the assistance: inscriptions however to commemorate a departed friend, are evidently exempt from the censure; the monuments would be unintelligible without them; and an urn, in a lonely grove, or in the midst of a field, is a favourite embellishment at the Leasowes; they are indeed among the principal ornaments of the place; for the buildings are mostly mere seats, or little root-houses; a ruin of a priory is the largest, and that has no peculiar beauty to recommend it; but a multiplicity of objects are unnecessary in the farm; the country it commands is full of them; and every natural advantage of the place within itself has been discovered, applied, contrasted, and carried to the utmost perfection, in the purest taste, and with inexhaustible fancy.

Among the ideas of pastoral poetry which are here introduced, its mythology is not omitted; but the allusions are both to ancient and to modern fables; sometimes to the fays and the fairies; and sometimes to the naiads and muses. The objects also are borrowed partly from the scenes which this country exhibited some centuries ago, and partly from those of Arcadia; the priory, and a Gothic seat, still more particularly characterised by an inscription in obsolete language and the black letter, belong to the one; the urns, Virgil's obelisk, and a rustic temple of Pan, to the other. All these allusions and objects are indeed equally rural; but the images in an English and a classical eclogue are not the same; each species is a distinct imitative character; either is proper; either will raise the farm it is applied to above the ordinary level; and within the compass of the same place both may be introduced; but they should be separate; when they are mixed, they counteract one another; and no representation is produced of the times and the countries they refer to. A certain district should therefore be allotted to each, that all the fields which belong to the respective characters may lie together; and the corresponding ideas be preserved for a continuance.

## LIII.

In such an assortment, the more open and polished scenes will generally be given to the Arcadian shepherd; and those in a lower degree of cultivation, will be thought more conformable to the *manners of the ancient British yeomanry*. We do not conceive that the country in their time was entirely cleared, or distinctly divided; the fields were surrounded by woods, not by hedges; and if a considerable tract of improved land lay together, it still was not separated into a number of inclosures. The subjects therefore proper to receive this character, are those in which cultivation seems to have encroached on the wild, not to have subdued it; as the bottom of a valley in corn, while the sides are still overgrown with wood; and the outline of that wood indented by the tillage creeping more or less up the hill. But a glade of grass thus circumstanced, does not peculiarly belong to the species; that may occur in a park or a pastoral farm: in this, the pastures should rather border on a waste or a common: if large, they may be broken by straggling bushes, thickets or coppices; and the scattered trees should be beset with brambles and briars. All these are circumstances which improve the beauty of the place, yet appear to be only remains of the wild, not intended for embellishment. Such interruptions must however be less frequent in the arable parts of the farm; but there the opening may be divided into several lands, distinguished, as in common fields, only by different sorts of grain. These will sufficiently break the sameness of the space; and tillage does not furnish a more pleasing scene, than such a space so broken, if the extent be moderate, and the boundary beautiful.

As much wood is essential to the character, a spot may easily be found, where turrets rising above the covert, or some arches seen within it, may have the resemblance of a castle or an abbey; the partial concealment is almost necessary to both; for to accord with the age, the buildings must seem to be entire; the ruins of them belong to later days: the disguise is however advantageous to them as objects; none can be imagined more picturesque, than a tower bosomed in trees, or a cloyster appearing between the stems and the branches. But the superstitions of the times furnish other objects, which are more within compass; hermitages were then real; solitary chapels were common; many of the springs of the country being deemed holy wells, were distinguished by little Gothic domes built over them; and every hamlet had its cross; even this, when perfect, set on a little rustic pillar, and that raised upon a base of circular steps, may in some scenes be considerable: if a situation can be found for a Maypole, whence it would not obtrude itself on every view, that also might not be improper; and an ancient church, however unwelcome it may be, when it breaks into the design of a park or a garden, in such a farm as this would be a fortunate accident; nor would the old yew in the church-yard be indifferent; it would be a memorial of the times when it was useful.

Many other objects, significant of the manners of our ancestors, might perhaps, upon recollection, occur; but these are amply sufficient for a place of considerable extent; and cottages must abound in every age and every country; they may therefore be introduced in different forms and positions. Large pieces of water are also particularly proper; and all the varieties of rills are consistent with every species of a farm. From the concurrence of so many agreable circumstances in this, be the force or the effect of the character what it may, a number of pleasing scenes may be exhibited either in a walk or riding, to be contrasted to those, which in another part of the place may be formed on Arcadian ideas; or even to be substituted in their stead, if they are omitted.

## LIV.

A part may also be free from either of these imitative characters, and laid out in a common simple farm; some of the greatest beauties of nature are to be found in the fields, and attend an ordinary state of cultivation; wood and water may there be exhibited in several forms and dispositions; we may enlarge or divide the inclosures, and give them such shapes and boundaries as we please; every one may be an agreeable spot; together they may compose beautiful views; the arable, the pasture, and the mead may succeed one another; and now and then a little wild may be intermixed without impropriety; every beauty, in short, which is not unusual in an enclosed country, whether it arise from neglect or improvement, is here in its place.

The buildings also which are frequent in such a country, are often beautiful objects; the church and the mansion are considerable; the farm-yard itself, if an advantageous situation be chosen for it; if the ricks, and the barns, and the outhouses are ranged with any design to form them into groupes; and they are properly blended with trees; may be made a picturesque composition. Many of them may be detached from the groupe, and dispersed about the grounds: the dove-cote, or the dairy, may be separated from the rest; they may be elegant in their forms, and placed where-ever they will have the best effect. A common barn, accompanied by a clump, is sometimes pleasing at a distance; a Dutch barn is so when near; and an hay-stack is generally an agreable circumstance in any position. Each of these may be single; and besides these, all kinds of cottages are proper. Among so many buildings, some may be converted to other purposes than their construction denotes; and whatever be their exterior, may within be made agreable retreats, for refreshment, indulgence, or shelter.

With such opportunities of improvement, even to decoration, within itself, and with advantages of prospect into the country about it, a simple farm may undoubtedly be delightful; it will be particularly acceptable to the owner, if it be close to his park or his garden; the objects which constantly remind him of his rank, impose a kind of constraint; and he feels himself relieved, by retiring sometimes from the splendor of a seat into the simplicity of a farm; it is more than a variety of scene; it is a temporary change of situation in life, which has all the charms of novelty, ease, and tranquillity, to recommend it. A place therefore can hardly be deemed perfect, which is not provided with such a retreat; but if it be the whole of the place, it seems inadequate to the mansion; a visitor is disappointed; the master is dissatisfied; he is not sufficiently distinguished from his tenants; he misses the appendages incidental to his seat and his fortune; and is hurt at the similarity of his grounds with the country about them. A pastoral or an ancient farm is a little above the common level; but even these, if brought close up to the door, set the house in a field, where it always appears to be neglected and naked. Some degree of polish and ornament is expected in its immediate environs; and a garden, though it be but a small one, should be interposed between the mansion and any species of farm.

### LV.

A sense of the propriety of such improvements about a seat, joined to a taste for the more simple delights of the country, probably suggested the idea of an *ornamented farm*, as the means of bringing every rural circumstance within the verge of a garden. This idea has been partially executed very often; but no where, I believe, so completely, and to such an extent, as at *Woburn farm. The place contains an hundred and fifty acres, of which near five and thirty are adorned to the highest degree; of the rest, about two thirds are in pasture, and the remainder is in tillage: the decorations are, however, communicated to every part; for they are disposed along the sides of a walk, which, with

---

* Belonging to Mrs. Southcote, near Weybridge in Surry.

its appendages, forms a broad belt round the grazing grounds; and is continued, though on a more contracted scale, through the arable. This walk is properly garden; all within it is farm; the whole lies on the two sides of a hill, and on a flat at the foot of it: the flat is divided into corn-fields; the pastures occupy the hill; they are surrounded by the walk, and crossed by a communication carried along the brow, which is also richly dressed, and which divides them into two lawns, each completely encompassed with garden.

These are in themselves delightful; the ground in both lies beautifully; they are diversified with clumps and single trees; and the buildings in the walk seem to belong to them. On the top of the hill is a large octagon structure; and not far from it, the ruin of a chapel. To one of the lawns the ruin appears, on the brow of a gentle ascent, backed and grouped with wood; from the other is seen the octagon, upon the edge of a steep fall, and by the side of a pretty grove, which hangs down the declivity. This lawn is further embellished by a neat Gothic building; the former by the house, and the lodge at the entrance; and in both, other objects of less consequence, little seats, alcoves, and bridges, continually occur.

The buildings are not, however, the only ornaments of the walk; it is shut out from the country, for a considerable length of the way, by a thick and lofty hedge-row, which is enriched with woodbine, jessamine, and every odoriferous plant, whose tendrils will entwine with the thicket. A path, generally of sand or gravel, is conducted in a waving line, sometimes close under the hedge, sometimes at a little distance from it; and the turf on either hand is diversified with little groupes of shrubs, of firs, or the smallest trees, and often with beds of flowers; these are rather too profusely strewed, and hurt the eye by their littlenesses; but then they replenish the air with their perfumes, and every gale is full of fragrancy. In some parts, however, the decoration is more chaste; and the walk is

carried between larger clumps of evergreens, thickets of deciduous shrubs, or still more considerable open plantations. In one
place it is entirely simple, without any appendages, any gravel,
or any sunk fence to separate it from the lawn, and is distinguished only by the richness of its verdure, and the nicety of
its preservation: in the arable part it is also of greenswerd, following the direction of the hedges about the several enclosures;
these hedges are sometimes thickened with flowering shrubs;
and in every corner, or vacant space, is a rosary, a close or an
open clump, or a bed of flowers: but if the parterre has been
rifled for the embellishment of the fields, the country has on
the other hand been searched for plants new in a garden; and
the shrubs and the flowers which used to be deemed peculiar
to the one, have been liberally transferred to the other; while
their number seems multiplied by their arrangement in so many
and such different dispositions. A more moderate use of them
would, however, have been better, and the variety more pleasing, had it been less licentious.

But the excess is only in the borders of the walk; the scenes
through which it leads are truly elegant, every where rich, and
always agreable. A peculiar chearfulness overspreads both the
lawns, arising from the number and the splendor of the objects with which they abound, the lightness of the buildings,
the inequalities of the ground, and the varieties of the plantations. The clumps and the groves, through separately small,
are often massed by the perspective, and gathered into considerable groupes, which are beautiful in their forms, their tints,
and their positions. The brow of the hill commands two lovely
prospects; the one gay and extensive, over a fertile plain, watered by the Thames, and broken by St. Ann's Hill, and Windsor Castle; a large mead, of the most luxuriant verdure, lies just
below the eye, spreading to the banks of the river; and beyond it
the country is full of farms, villas, and villages, and every mark
of opulence and cultivation. The other view is more wooded;

the steeple of a church, or the turrets of a seat, sometimes rise above the trees; and the bold arch of Walton Bridge is there a conspicuous object, equally singular and noble. The enclosures on the flat are more retired and quiet; each is confined within itself; and all together they form an agreable contrast to the open exposure above them.

With the beauties which enliven a garden, are every where intermixed many properties of a farm; both the lawns are fed; and the lowings of the herds, the bleating of the sheep, and the tinklings of the bell-wether, resound thro' all the plantations; even the clucking of poultry is not omitted; for a menagerie of a very simple design is placed near the Gothic building; a small serpentine river is provided for the water-fowl; while the others stray among the flowering shrubs on the banks, or straggle about the neighbouring lawn: and the corn fields are the subjects of every rural employment, which arable land, from seed-time to harvest, can furnish. But though so many of the circumstances occur, the simplicity of a farm is wanting; that idea is lost in such a profusion of ornament; a rusticity of character cannot be preserved amidst all the elegant decorations which may be lavished on a garden.

# Of a PARK.

## LVI.

A *park* and a garden are more nearly allied, and can therefore be accommodated to each other, without any disparagement to either. A farm loses some of its characteristic properties by the connexion, and the advantage is on the part of the garden; but a park thus bordered, retains all its own excellencies; they are only enriched, not counteracted, by the intermixture. The most perfect composition of a place that can be imagined, consists of a garden opening into a park, with a short walk through the latter to a farm, and ways along its glades to ridings in the country; but to the farm and the ridings the park is no more than a passage; and its woods and its buildings are but circumstances in their views; its scenes can be communicated only to the garden.

The affinity of the two subjects is so close, that it would be difficult to draw the exact line of separation between them: gardens have lately encroached very much both in extent and in style on the character of a park; but still there are scenes in the one, which are out of the reach of the other; the small sequestered spots which are agreeable in a garden, would be trivial in a park; and the spacious lawns which are among the noblest features of the latter, would in the former fatigue by their want of variety; even such as being of a moderate extent may be admitted into either, will seem bare and naked, if not broken in the one; and lose much of their greatness, if broken in the other. The proportion of a part to the whole, is a measure of its dimensions: it often determines the proper size for an object, as well as the space fit to be allotted to a scene; and regulates the style which ought to be assigned to either.

But whatever distinctions the extent may occasion between a park and a garden, a state of highly cultivated nature is consistent with each of their characters; and may in both be of the same kind, though in different degrees. The same species of preservation, of ornament, and of scenery, may be introduced; and though a large portion of a park may be rude; and the most romantic scenes are not incompatible with its character; yet it should seem rather to be reclaimed from a forest, than a neglected corner of it; the wildness must not be universal; it is but a circumstance; and it is a happy circumstance only when it is kept within due bounds; some appearance of improvement is essential; and a high degree of polish is at times expected, and generally agreable. All scenes wherein it prevails, naturally coalesce; the roughness of others is softened by distance; and even these, when near, may be noble views, though too vast and too wild to be parts of a garden. On the other hand, the minute beauties of a walk, when seen across a spacious lawn, are combined into large masses, and by their number amount to greatness. As a park, therefore, and a garden, agree in so many circumstances, and may by the point of view be accommodated to each other in those wherein they principally differ, frequent opportunities must occur to form an intimate union between them.

Painshill* is situated on the utmost verge of a moor, which rises above a fertile plain, watered by the Mole. Large vallies descending in different directions towards the river, break the brow into separate eminences; and the gardens are extended along the edge, in a semi-circular form, between the winding river which describes their outward boundary, and the park which fills up the cavity of the crescent: the moor lies behind the place, and sometimes appears too conspicuously; but the views on the other sides into the cultivated country are agreable; they are terminated by hills at a competent distance; the plain is sufficient varied with objects; and the richest meadows overspread the bottom just below: the prospects are, however, only pretty, not fine; and the river is languid and dull. Painshill, therefore, is little benefited by external circumstances; but the scenes within itself are both grand and beautiful; and the disposition of the gardens affords frequent opportunities of seeing the several parts, the one from the other, across the park, in a variety of advantageous situations.

The house stands at one extremity of the crescent, on a hill which is shut out from the park, but open to the country. The view is chearful; and the spot is laid out in an elegant garden taste, pretending to no more than to be pleasant. In the midst

* The seat of Mr. Hamilton, near Cobham in Surry.

of the thicket which separates it from the park, is a parterre, and an orangerie, where the exotic plants are, during the summer, intermixed with common shrubs, and a constant succession of flowers. The space before the house is full of ornament; the ground is prettily varied; and several sorts of beautiful trees are disposed on the sides in little open plantations.

This hill is divided from another much larger by a small valley; and on the top of the second eminence, at a seat just above a large vineyard which overspreads all the side, a scene totally different appears: the general prospect, though beautiful, is the circumstance the least engaging; the attention is immediately attracted from the cultivated plain, to the point of a hanging wood at a distance, but still within the place, and which is not only a noble object in itself, but affords the most pleasing encouragement to all who delight in gardening; for it has been raised by the present possessor; and by its situation, its thickness, and extent, while it retains the freshness of a young plantation, has already in appearance all the massy richness of an old one. Opposite to the hill thus covered, is another in the country, of a similar shape, but bare and barren; and beyond the opening between them, the moor falling back into a wide concave, closes the interval. Had all these heights belonged to the same proprietor, and being planted in the same manner, they would have composed as great, as romantic a scene, as any of those which we rarely see, but always behold with admiration, the work of nature alone, matured by the growth of ages.

But Painshill is all a new creation; and a boldness of design, and a happiness of execution, attend the wonderful efforts which art has there made to rival nature. Another point of the same eminence exhibits a landskip distinguished from the last in every particular, except in the aera of its existence: it is entirely within the place; and commanded from an open Gothic building, on the very edge of a high steep, which rises immediately above a fine artificial lake in the bottom: the whole of this lake is never seen at once; but by its form, by the disposition of some islands, and by the trees in them and on the banks, it always seems to be larger than it is: on the left are continued plantations, to exclude the country; on the right, all the park opens; and in front, beyond the water, is the hanging wood, the point of which appeared before, but here it stretches quite across the view, and displays all its extent, and all its varieties. A broad river, issuing from the lake, passes under a bridge of five arches near the outlet, then directs its course towards the wood, and flows underneath it. On the side of the hill is couched a low hermitage, encompassed with thicket, and overhung with shade; and far to the right, on the utmost summit, rises a lofty tower, eminent above all the trees. About the hermitage, the closest covert, and the darkest greens, spread their gloom: in other places the tints are mixed; and in one, a little glimmering light marks an opening in the wood, and diversifies its uniformity, without diminishing its greatness. Throughout the illustrious scene consistency is preserved in the midst of variety; all the parts unite easily; the plantations in the bottom join to the wood which hangs on the hill; those on the upper grounds of the park, break into groves, which afterwards divide into clumps, and in the end taper into single trees. The ground is very various, but it points from all sides towards the lake, and slackening its descent as it approaches, slides at last gently into the water. The groves and the lawns on the declivities are elegant and rich; the fine expanse of the lake, enlivened by the gay plantations on the banks, and the reflection of the bridge upon the surface, animates the landskip; and the extent and the height of the hanging wood give an air of grandeur to the whole.

An easy winding descent leads from the Gothic building to the lake, and a broad walk is afterwards continued along the banks, and across an island, close to the water on one hand, and skirted by wood on the other: the spot is perfectly retired;

but the retirement is chearful; the lake is calm; but it is full to the brim, and never darkened with shadow; the walk is smooth, and almost level, and touches the very margin of the water; the wood, which secludes all view into the country, is composed of the most elegant trees, full of the lightest greens, and bordered with shrubs and with flowers; and though the place is almost surrounded with plantations, yet within itself it is open and airy; it is embellished with three bridges, a ruined arch, and a grotto; and the Gothic building, still very near, and impending directly over the lake, belongs to the place; but these objects are never visible all together; they appear in succession as the walk proceeds; and their number does not croud the scene which is enriched by their frequency.

The transition is very sudden, almost immediate, from this polished spot, to another of the most uncultivated nature; not dreary, not romantic, but rude; it is a wood, which overspreads a large tract of very uneven ground; the glades through it are just cleared of the bushes and plants, which are natural to the soil; sometimes they are closed on both sides with thickets; at other times they are only cut through the fern in the openings; and even the larches, and the firs, which are mixed with beech on the side of the principal glade, are left in such a state of apparent neglect, that they seem to be the product of the wild, not decorations of the walk: this is the hanging wood, which before was so noble an object, and is now such a distant retreat; near the tower it is thin; but about the hermitage it is thickened with trees of the darkest greens; a narrow gloomy path, overhung with Scotch and spruce firs, under which the fern seems to have been killed, not cleared, and scarce a blade of grass can grow, leads to the cell; that is composed of logs and of roots; the design is as simple as the materials; and the furniture within is old and uncouth; all the circumstances which belong to the character, are retained in the utmost purity, both in the approach and the entrance; in the second room they are suddenly changed for a view of the gardens and the country, which is rich with every appearance of inhabitants and cultivation. From the tower on the top of the hill is another prospect, much more extensive, but not more beautiful; the objects are not so well selected, not seen to so great advantage; some of them are too distant; some too much below the eye; and a large portion of the heath intervenes, which casts a cloud over the view.

Not far from the tower is a scene polished to the highest degree of improvement, in which stands a large Doric building, called the temple of Bacchus, with a fine portico in the front, a rich alto relievo in the pediment, and on each side a range of pilasters: within, it is decorated with many antique busts, and a noble statue of the god in the centre; the room has none of that solemnity which is often affectedly ascribed to the character, but without being gaudy is full of light, of ornament, and splendor; the situation is on a brow, which commands an agreeable prospect; but the top of the hill is almost a flat, diversified however by several thickets, and broad walks winding between them; these walks run into each other so frequently, their relation is so apparent that the idea of the whole is never lost in the divisions; and the parts are, like the whole, large; they agree also in style; the interruptions therefore never destroy the appearance of extent; they only change the boundaries, and multiply the figures: to the grandeur which the spot receives from such dimensions, is added all the richness of which plantations are capable; the thickets are of flowering shrubs; and the openings are embellished with little airy groupes of the most elegant trees, skirting or crossing the glades; but nothing is minute, or unworthy of the environs of the temple.

The gardens end here; this is one of the extremities of the crescent, and from hence to the house in the other extremity, is an open walk through the park; in the way a tent is pitched, upon a fine swell, just above the water, which is seen to greater advantage from this point than from any other; its broadest expanse is at the foot of the hill; from that it spreads in several directions, sometimes under the plantations, sometimes into the midst of them, and at other times winding behind them; the principal bridge of five arches is just below; at a distance, deep in the wood, is another, a single arch, thrown over a stream which is lost a little beyond it; the position of the latter is directly athwart that of the former; the eye passes along the one, and under the other; and the greater is of stone, the smaller of wood; no two objects bearing the same name, can be more different in figure and situation: the banks also of the lake and infinitely diversified; they are open in one place, and in another covered with plantations; which sometimes come down to the brink of the water; and sometimes leave room for a walk; the glades are either conducted along the sides, or open into the thickest of the wood; and now and then they seem to turn round it towards the country, which appears in the offskip, rising above this picturesque and various scene, through a wide opening between the hanging wood on one hand, and the eminence crowned with the Gothic tower on the other.

## LVII.

Both the park and the gardens at Painshill thus mutually contribute to the beauty of the several landskips; yet they are absolutely distinct; and not only separated by fences very artfully concealed, but the character of each is preserved pure in the spots, from which the scenes wherein they mix are commanded. They may, however, be more closely united; and by transferring to the one, some of the circumstances which are usually, but not necessarily, confined to the other, they may be actually *blended* together. There are, indeed, properties in a garden, which cannot be applied to a park: its bloom and its fragrancy cannot there be preserved; if they could, the flowers, and the flowering shrubs, and the culture they require, would not assort with the place; even the more curious trees could hardly be secured from injuries; the little groupes, if raised, would seldom kindly coalesce with the woods of the forest around them; and several delicate finishings, and elegant ornaments, which become the confined spots of a garden, would, at the best, be lost in the larger scenes of a park. But still the latter may borrow many decorations from the former; and if the lawns and the woods be of a moderate extent, and great rather in style than in dimensions; if they be every where distinguished by elegance in their forms and their outlines; and if, in the communications between them, the appendages of a walk be preferred to those of a riding; the park may retain its own character; may be stocked with deer and with sheep, and amply provided with harbour and pasture; yet adopt, without any derogation, the capital beauties of a garden,

The excellencies both of a park and of a garden are thus happily blended at * Hagley, where the scenes are equally elegant and noble. It is situated in the midst of a fertile and lovely country, between the Clent and the Witchberry Hills, neither of which are within the pale, but both belong to the place. The latter rise in three beautiful swells; one of them is covered with wood; another is an open sheep-walk, with an obelisk on the summit; on the third, the portico of the temple of Theseus, exactly on the model of that at Athens, and little less in the dimensions, stand boldly out upon the brow, backed by the dark ground of a fir plantation, and has a most majestic appearance, above the steeps which fall before and beside it. The house is seen to the greatest advantage from these eminences, and every point of them commands some beautiful prospect; the busy town of Stourbridge is just below them; the ruins of Dudley castle rise in the offskip; the country is full of industry and inhabitants; and a small portion of the moor, where the minerals, manufactured

---

* Near Stourbridge, in Worcestershire.

in the neighbourhood, are dug, breaking in upon the horizon, accounts for the richness, without derogating from the beauty of the landskip. From the Clent hills the views are still greater; they extend on one side to the black mountains in Wales, a long ridge which appears, at sixty miles distance, in the interval between the unwieldy heap of the Malvern hills, and the solitary peak of the Wrekin, each thirty miles off, and as many asunder. The smoak of Worcester, the churches in Birmingham, and the houses in Stourbridge, are distinctly visible; the country is a mixture of hill and dale, and strongly enclosed, except in one part, where a heath, varied by rising grounds, pieces of water, and several objects, forms an agreable contrast to the cultivation which surrounds it. From the other extremity of the Clent hills, the prospect is less extensive; but the ground is more rude and broken; it is often overspread with large and beautiful woods; and the view is dignified with numerous seats: the hills also being very irregular, large advanced promontories frequently interrupt the sight, and vary the scene: in other parts, deep vallies shelving down towards the country below, exhibit the objects there in different lights. In one of these hollows is built a neat cottage, under a deep descent, sheltered besides by plantations, and presenting ideas of retirement in the midst of so much open exposure; from the heights above it, is seen all that view which before was commanded from the Witchberry hills, but which is seen here over Hagley Park, a noble foreground, beautiful in itself, and completing the landskip.

The house, though low in the park, is yet above the adjacent country, which it overlooks to a very distant horizon: it is surrounded by a lawn, of fine uneven ground, and diversified with large clumps, little groupes, and single trees; it is open in front, but covered on one side by the Witchberry hills; on the other side, and behind, by the eminences in the park, which are high and steep, and all overspread with a lofty hanging wood. The lawn pressing to the foot, or creeping up the slopes of these hills, and sometimes winding along glades into the depth of the wood, traces a beautiful outline to a sylvan scene, already rich to luxuriance in massiness of foliage, and stateliness of growth.

But though the wood appears to be entire, it in reality opens frequently into lawns, which occupy much of the space within it: in the number, the variety, and the beauty of these lawns, in the shades of the separations between them, in their beauties also, and their varieties, the glory of Hagley consists; no two of the openings are alike, in dimensions, in shape, or in character; one is of no more than five or six acres; another of not less than fifty; and others are of all the intermediate sizes; some stretch out into lengthened glades; some widen every way; they are again distinguished by buildings, by prospects, and often by the style only of the plantations around them. The boundary of one is described by a few careless lines; that of another is composed of many parts, very different and very irregular; and the ground is never flat, but falls sometimes in steep descents, sometimes in gentle declivities, waves along easy swells, or is thrown into broken inequalities, with endless variety.

An octagon seat, sacred to the memory of Tomson, and erected on his favourite spot, stands on the brow of a steep; a mead winds along the valley beneath, till it is lost on either hand behind some trees; opposite to the seat, a noble wood crowns the top, and feathers down to the bottom, of a large, oval, swelling hill; as it descends on one side, the distant country becomes the offskip; over the fall on the other side the Clent hills appear; a dusky antique tower stands just below them, at the extremity of the wood; and in the midst of it is seen a Doric portico, called Pope's Building, with part of the lawn before it; the scene is very simple; the principal features are great; they prevail over all the rest, and are intimately connected with each other.

The next opening is small, circling about a rotunda on a knole, to the foot of which the ground rises every way; the trees which surround it are large; but their foliage is not very thick;

and their stems appearing beneath, their ramifications between, the boughs, are, in so confined a spot, very distinguished and agreable circumstances: it is retired; has no prospect; no visible outlet but one, and that is short and narrow, to a bridge with a portico upon it, which terminates a piece of water.

The grove behind the rotunda, separates this from a large, airy, forest glade, thinly skirted with wood, careless of dress, and much overgrown with fern. The wildness is an acceptable relief in the midst of so much elegance and improvement as reign in the neighbouring lawns; and the place is in itself pleasant; in no part confined; and from a Gothic seat at the end is a perspective view of that wood and tower, which were seen before in front, together with the Witchberry hills, and a wide range of country.

The tower, which in prospect is always connected with wood, stands however on a piece of down, which stretches along the broad ridge of a hill, and spreads on each hand for some way down the sides: thick groves catch the falls; the descent on the right is soon lost under the trees; but that on the left being steeper and shorter, it may be followed to the bottom; a wood hangs on the declivity, which is continued in the valley beneath; the tower overlooks the whole; it seems the remains of a castle, partly entire, partly in ruins, and partly overgrown with bushes; a finer situation cannot be imagined; it is placed in an exposed unfrequented spot; commands an extensive prospect; and is every where an interesting object.

At the end of the valley below it, in an obscure corner, and shut out from all view, is a hermitage, composed of roots and of moss; high banks, and a thick covert darkened with horse-chesnuts, confine the sequestered spot; a little rill trickles through it, and two small pieces of water occupy the bottom; they are seen on one side through groupes of trees; the other is open, but covered with fern: this valley is the extremity of the park, and the Clent hills rise in all their irregularity immediately above it.

The other descent from the castle is a long declivity, covered like the rest with noble woods, in which fine lawns are again embosomed, differing still from the former, and from each other: in one, the ground is very rough, the boundary is much broken, and marked only by the trunks of the trees which shoot up high before the branches begin. The next is more simple; and the ground falls from an even brow into one large hollow, which slopes towards the glen, where it sinks into the covert. This has a communication through a short glade, and between two groves, with another, called the Tinian lawn, from the resemblance which it is said to bear to those of that celebrated island; it is encompassed with the stateliest trees, all fresh and vigorous, and so full of leaf that not a stem, not a branch, appears, but large masses or foliage only describe an undulating outline: the effect however is not produced by the boughs feathering down to the bottom; they in appearance shoot out horizontally a few feet above the ground to a surprizing distance, and form underneath an edging of shade, into which the retreat is immediate at every hour of the day; the verdure of the turf is as luxuriant there as in the open space; the ground gently waves in both over easy swells and little dips, just varying, not breaking the surface; no strong lines are drawn; no striking objects are admitted; but all is of an even temper, all mild, placid, and serene, in the gayest season of the day not more than chearful, in the stillest watch of night not gloomy; the scene is indeed peculiarly adapted to the tranquility of the latter, when the moon seems to repose her light on the thick foliage of the grove, and steadily marks the shade of every bough; it is delightful then to saunter here, and see the grass, and the gossamer which entwines it, glistening with dew; to listen and hear nothing stir, except perhaps a withered leaf dropping gently through a tree; and sheltered from the chill, to catch the freshness of the evening air: a solitary urn, chosen by Mr. Pope for the spot, and now inscribed to his memory, when shewn by a gleam of moon-light through the trees, fixes that thoughtfulness and composure, to which the mind is insensibly led by the rest of this elegant scene.

The Doric Portico which also bears his name, though not within sight is near; it is placed on the declivity of a hill; and Tomson's seat, with its groves and appendages, are agreable circumstances in the prospect before it. In the valley beneath is fixed a bench, which commands a variety of short views; one is up the ascent to the portico, and others through openings in the wood to the bridge and the rotunda.

The next lawn is large; the ground is steep and irregular, but inclines to one direction, and falls from every side into the general declivity; the outline is diversified by many groupes of trees on the slopes; and frequent glimpses of the country are seen in perspective through openings between them: on the brow is a seat, in the proudest situation of all Hagley; it commands a view down the bold sweep of the lawn, and over a valley filled with the noblest trees, up to the heights beyond; one of those heights is covered with a hanging wood; which opens only to shew Tomson's seat, and the groves, and the steeps about it; the others are the Witchberry hills, which seems to press forward into the landskip; and the massy heads of the trees in the vale, uniting into a continued surface, form a broad base to the temple of Theseus, hide the swell on which it is built, and croud up to the very foundation; farther back stands the obelisk; before it is the sheep-walk; behind it the Witchberry wood: the temple is backed by the firs; and both these plantations are connected with that vast sylvan scene, which overspreads the other hill, and all the intermediate valley; such extent of wood; such variety in the disposition of it; objects so illustrious in themselves, and ennobled by their situations, each contrasted to each, every one distinct, and all happily united: the parts so beautiful of a whole so great; seen from a charming lawn; and surrounded by a delightful country; compose all together a scene of real magnificence and grandeur.

The several lawns are separated by the finest trees; which sometimes grow in airy groves, chequered with gleams of light, and open to every breeze; but more frequently, whose great branches meeting or crossing each other, cast a deep impenetrable shade. Large boughs feathering down often intercept the sight; or a vacant space is filled with coppice wood, nut, hawthorn, and hornbeam, whose tufted heads mixing with the foliage, and whose little stems clustering about the trunks of the trees, thicken and darken the plantation; here and there the division is of such coppice wood only, which then being less constrained and oppressed, springs up stronger, spreads further, and joins in a low vaulted covering; in other places the shade is high over-arched by the tallest ash, or spreads under the branches of the most venerable oaks; they rise in every shape, they are disposed in every form, in which trees can grow; the ground beneath them is sometimes almost level; sometimes a gentle swell; but generally very irregular and broken: in several places, large hollows wind down the sides of the hills, worn in the stormy months by water-courses, but worn many ages ago; very old oaks in the midst of the channels prove their antiquity: some of them are perfectly dry most part of the year; and some are watered by little rills all the summer; they are deep and broad; the sides are commonly steep; often abrupt and hollow; and the trees on the bank sometimes extend their roots, all covered with moss, over the channels of the water. Low down in one of these glens, under a thick shade of horse-chesnuts, is a plain bench, in the midst of several little currents, and water-falls, running among large loose stones, and the stumps of dead trees, with which the ground is broken: on the brink of another glen, which is distinguished by a numerous rookery, is a seat in a still wilder situation, near a deeper hollow, and in a darker gloom; the falls are nearly perpendicular; the roots of some of the trees are almost bare, from the earth having crumbled away; large boughs of others, sinking with their own weight, seem ready to break from the trunks they belong to; and the finest ash, still growing, lie all aslant the water-course below, which, though the stream runs in winter only, yet constantly retains the black tinge of damp, and casts a chill all around.

Gravel walks are conducted across the glens, through the woods, the groves, or the thickets, and along the sides of the lawns, concealed generally from the sight, but always ready for the communication; and leading to the principal scenes; the frequency of these walks, the number and the style of the buildings, and the high preservation in which all the place is kept, give to the whole park the air of a garden; there is however one spot more peculiarly adapted to that purpose, and more artificially disposed than the rest; it is a narrow vale, divided into three parts; one of them is quite filled with water, which leaves no room for a path, but thick trees on either side come down quite to the brink; and between them the sight is conducted to the bridge with a portico upon it, which closes the view: another part of this vale is a deep gloom, over-hung with large ash, and oaks, and darkened below by a number of yews; these are scattered over very uneven ground, and open underneath; but they are encompassed by a thick covert, under which a stream falls, from a stony channel, down a rock; other rills drop into the current, which afterwards pours over a second cascade into the third division of the vale, where it forms a piece of water, and is lost under the bridge: the view from this bridge is a perfect opera scene, through all the divisions of the vale, up to the rotunda; both these buildings, and the other decorations of the spot, are of the species generally confined to a garden; the hermitage also, which has been described, and its appendages, are in a stile which does not belong to a park; but through all the rest of the place, the two characters are intimately blended; the whole is one subject; and it was a bold idea to conceive that one to be capable of so much variety; it required the most vigorous efforts of a fertile fancy to carry that idea into execution.

## Of a GARDEN.

## LVIII.

The gravel paths have been mentioned as contributing to the appearance of a garden; they are unusual elsewhere; they constantly present the idea of a walk; and the correspondence between their sides, the exactness of the edges, the nicety of the materials and of the preservation, appropriate them to spots in the highest state of improvement: applied to any other subject than a park, their effect is the same; a field surrounded by a gravel walk is to a degree bordered by a garden; and many ornaments may be introduced as appendages to the latter, which would otherwise appear to be inconsistent with the former; when these accompaniments occupy a considerable space, and are separated from the field, the idea of a garden is complete as far as they extend; but if the gravel be omitted, and the walk be only of turf, a greater breadth to the border, and more richness in the decorations, are necessary, to preserve that idea.

Many gardens are nothing more than such *a walk round a field*; that field is often raised to the character of a lawn; and sometime the enclosure is, in fact, a paddock; whatever it be, the walk is certainly garden; it is a spot set apart for pleasure; it admits on the sides a profusion of ornament; it is fit for the reception of every elegance; and requires the nicest preservation; it is attended also with many advantages; may be made and kept without much expence; leads to a variety of points; and avails itself in its progress of the several circumstances which belong to the enclosure it surrounds, whether they be the rural appurtenances of a farm, or those more refined which distinguish a paddock.

But it has at the same time its inconveniencies and defects: its approach to the several points is always circuitous, and they are thereby often thrown to a distance from the house, and from each other; there is no access to them across the open exposure; the way must constantly be the same; the view all along is into one opening, which must be peculiarly circumstanced, to furnish within itself a sufficient variety; and the embellishments of the walk are seldom important; their number is limited, and the little space allotted for their reception admits only of those which can be accommodated to the scale, and will conform to the character. This species of garden, therefore, reduces almost to a sameness all the places it is applied to; the subject seems exhausted; no walk round a field can now be very different from several others already existing. At the best too it is but a walk; the fine scenery of a garden is wanting; and that in the field, which is substituted in its stead, is generally of an inferior character; and often defective in connection with the spot which commands it, by the intervention of the fence, or the visible difference in the preservation.

This objection, however, has more or less force according to the character of the enclosure: if that be a paddock or a lawn, it may exhibit scenes not unworthy of the most elegant garden, which agreeing in style, will unite in appearance, with the walk. The other objections also are stronger or weaker in proportion to the space allowed for the appendages; and not applicable at all to a broad circuit of garden, which has room within itself for scenery, variety, and character; but the common narrow walk, too indiscriminately in fashion, if continued to a considerable extent, becomes very tiresome; and the points it leads to must be more than ordinarily delightful, to compensate for the fatigue of the way.

This tediousness may, however, be remedied, without any extravagant enlargement of the plan, by taking in, at certain intervals, an additional breadth, sufficient only for a little scene to interrupt the uniformity of the progress. The walk is then a communication, not between points of view, through all which it remains unaltered; but between the several parts of a garden, in each of which it is occasionally lost; and when resumed, it is at the worst a repetition, not a continuation of the same idea; the eye and the mind are not always confined to one tract; they expatiate at times, and have been relieved before they return to it. Another expedient, the very reverse of this, may now and then be put in practice: it is to contract, instead of enlarging, the plan; to carry the walk, in some part of its course, directly into the field; or at the most to secure it from cattle; but to make it quite simple, omit all its appendages, and drop every idea of a garden. If neither of these, nor any other means be used to break the length of the way, though the enclosures should furnish a succession of scenes, all beautiful, and even contrasted to each other, yet the walk will introduce a similarity between them. This species of garden, therefore, seems proper only for a place of a very moderate extent; if it be stretched out to a great length, and not mixed with other characters, its sameness hurts that variety, which it is its peculiar merit to discover.

## LIX.

But the advantages attending it upon some, and the use of it on so many occasions, have raised a partiality in its favour; and it is often carried round a place, where *the whole enclosure is garden*; the interior openings and communications furnish there a sufficient range; and they do not require that number and variety of appendages, which must be introduced to disguise the uniformity of the circuitous walk, but which often interfere with greater effects. It is at the least unnecessary in such a garden; but plain gravel walks to every part are commonly deemed to be indispensable; they undoubtedly are convenient; but it must also be acknowledged, that though sometimes they adorn, yet at other times they disfigure the scenes through which they are conducted. The proprietor of the place, who visits these scenes at different seasons, is most anxious for their beauty in fine weather; he does not feel the restraint to be grievous, if all of them be not at all times equally accessible; and a gravel walk perpetually before him, especially when it is useless, must be irksome; it ought not, therefore, to be ostentatiously shewn; on many occasions it should be industriously concealed; that it lead to the capital points is sufficient; it can never be requisite along the whole extent of every scene; it may often skirt a part of them, without appearing; or just touch upon them, and withdraw; but if it cannot be introduced at all without hurting them, it ought commonly to be omitted.

The sides of a gravel walk must correspond, and its course be in sweeps gently bending all the way. It preserves its form, though conducted through woods, or along glades, of the most licentious irregularity; but a grass walk is under no restraint; the sides of it may be perpetually broken; and the direction frequently changed; sudden turns, however, are harsh; they check the idea of progress; they are rather disappointments than varieties; and if they are similar, they are in the worst style of affectation. The line must be curved, but it should not be wreathed; if it be truly serpentine, it is the most unnatural of any; it ought constantly to proceed; and wind only just so much, that the termination of the view may differ at every step, and the end of the walk never appear; the thickets which confine it should be diversified with several mixtures of greens; no distinctions in the forms of the shrubs or the trees will be lost, when there are opportunities to observe them so nearly; and combinations and contrasts without number may be made, which will be there truly ornamental. Minute beauties are proper in a spot precluded from great effects; and yet such a walk, if it be broad, is by no means insignificant; it may have an importance which will render it more than a mere communication.

But the peculiar merit of that species of garden, which occupies the whole enclosure, consists in the larger scenes; it can make room for them both in breadth and in length; and being dedicated entirely to pleasure, free from all other considerations, those scenes may be in any style which the nature of the place will allow; a number of them is expected; all different; sometimes contrasted; and each distinguished by its beauty. If the space be divided into little slips, and made only a collection of walks, it forfeits all its advantages, loses its character, and can have no other excellence than such as it may derive from situation; whereas by a more liberal disposition, it may be made independent of whatever is external; and though prospects are no where more delightful than from a point of view which is also a beautiful spot, yet if in such a garden they should be wanting, the elegant, picturesque, and various scenes within itself, almost supply the deficiency.

This is the character of the gardens at Stowe: for there the views in the country are only circumstances subordinate to the scenes; and the principal advantage of the situation is the variety of the ground within the enclosure. The house stands on the brow of a gentle ascent; part of the gardens lie on the declivity, and spread over the bottom beyond it; this eminence is separated by a broad winding valley from another which is higher and steeper; and the descents of both are broken by large dips and hollows, sloping down the sides of the hills. The whole space is divided into a number of scenes, each distinguished with taste and fancy; and the changes are so frequent, so sudden, and complete, the transitions so artfully conducted, that the same ideas are never continued or repeated to satiety.

These gardens were begun when regularity was in fashion; and the original boundary is still preserved, on account of its magnificence; for round the whole circuit, of between three and four miles, is carried a very broad gravel walk, planted with rows of trees, and open either to the park or the country; a deep-sunk fence attends it all the way, and comprehends a space of near four hundred acres. But in the interior scenes of the garden, few traces of regularity appear; where it yet remains in the plantations, it is generally disguised; every symptom almost of formality is obliterated from the ground; and an octagon basin in the bottom, is now converted into an irregular piece of water, which receives on one hand two beautiful streams, and falls on the other down a cascade into a lake.

In the front of the house is a considerable lawn, open to the water, beyond which are two elegant Doric pavillions, placed in the boundary of the garden, but not marking it, though they correspond to each other; for still further back, on the brow of some rising grounds without the enclosure, stands a noble Corinthian arch, by which the principal approach is conducted, and from which all the gardens are seen, reclining back against their hills; they are rich with plantations, full of objects, and lying on both sides of the house almost equally, every part is within a moderate distance, notwithstanding the extent of the whole.

On the right of the lawn, but concealed from the house, is a perfect garden scene, called the queen's amphitheatre, where art is avowed, though formality is avoided; the fore-ground is scooped into a gentle hollow; the plantations on the sides, though but just rescued from regularity, yet in style are contrasted to each other; they are, on one hand, chiefly thickets, standing out from a wood; on the other, they are open groves, through which a glimpse of the water is visible: at the end of the hollow, on a little knole, quite detached from all appendages, is placed an open Ionic rotunda; beyond it, a large lawn slopes across the view; a pyramid stands on the brow; the queen's pillar, in a recess on the descent; and all the three buildings being evidently intended for ornament alone, are peculiarly adapted to a garden scene; yet their number does not render it gay; the dusky hue of the pyramid, the retired situation of the queen's pillar, and the solitary appearance of the rotunda, give it an air of gravity; it is encompassed with wood; and all external views are excluded; even the opening into the lawn is but an opening into an enclosure.

At the king's pillar, very near to this, is another lovely spot; which is small, but not confined; for no termination appears; the ground one way, the water another, retire under the trees out of sight, but no where meet with a boundary; the view is first over some very broken ground, thinly and irregularly planted; then between two beautiful clumps, which feather down to the bottom; and afterwards across a glade, and through a little grove beyond it, to that part of the lake, where the thickets, close upon the brink, spread a tranquility over the surface, in which their shadows are reflected: nothing is admitted to disturb that quiet; no building obtrudes; for objects to fix the eye are needless in a scene, which may be comprehended at a glance; and none would suit the pastoral idea it inspires, of elegance too refined for a cottage, and of simplicity too pure for any other edifice.

The situation of the rotunda promises a prospect more enlarged; and in fact most of the objects on this side of the garden, are there visible; but they want both connection and contrast; each belongs peculiarly to some other spot; they are all blended together in this, without meaning; and are rather shewn on a map, than formed into a picture. The water only is capital; a broad expanse of it is so near as to be seen under the little groupes on the bank without interruption; beyond it is a wood, which in one place leaves the lake, to run up behind a beautiful building, of three pavillions, joined by arcades, all of the Ionic order; it is called Kent's Building; and never was a design more happily conceived; it seems to be characteristically proper for a garden; it is so elegant, so varied, and so purely ornamental; it directly fronts the rotunda, and a narrow rim of the country appears above the trees beyond it: but the effect even of this noble object is fainter here than at other points; its position is not the most advantageous; and it is but one among many other buildings, none of which are principal.

The scene at the temple of Bacchus is in character directly the reverse of that about the rotunda, though the space and the objects are nearly the same in both; but in this all the parts concur to form one whole; the ground from every side shelves gradually towards the lake; the plantations on the further bank open to shew Kent's building, rise from the water's edge towards the knole on which it stands, and close again behind it; that elegant structure, inclined a little from a front view, becomes more beautiful by being thrown into perspective; and though at a greater distance, is more important than before, because it is alone in the view: for the queen's pillar and the rotunda are removed far aside; and every other circumstance refers to this interesting object; the water attracts, the ground and the plantations direct the eye thither; and the country does not just glimmer in the offskip, but is close and eminent above the wood, and connected by clumps with the garden. The scene all together is a most animated landskip; and the splendor of the building; the reflection in the lake; the transparency of the water; and the picturesque beauty of its form, diversified by little groupes on the brink, while on the broadest expanse no more trees cast their shadows than are sufficient to vary the tints of the surface; all these circumstances, vying in lustre with each other, and uniting in the point to which every part of the scene is related, diffuse a peculiar brilliancy over the whole composition.

The view from Kent's building, is very different from those which have been hitherto described; they are all directed down the declivity of the lawn; this rises up the ascent; the eminence being crowned with lofty wood, becomes thereby more considerable; and the hillocks into which the general fall is broken, sloping further out this way than any other, they also acquire an importance which they had not before; that particularly on which the rotunda is placed, seems here to be a proud situation; and the structure appears to be properly adapted to so open an exposure. The temple of Bacchus on the contrary, which commands such an illustrious view, is itself a retired object, close under the covert: the wood rising on the brow, and descending down one side of the hill, is shewn to be deep; is high, and seems to be higher than it is; the lawn too is extensive; and part of the boundary being concealed, it suggests the idea of a still greater extent; a small portion only of the lake indeed is visible; but it is not here an object; it is a part of the spot; and neither termination being in sight, it has no diminutive appearance; if more water had been admitted, it might have hurt the character of the place, which is sober and temperate; neither solemn nor gay; great and simple, but elegant; above rusticity, yet free from ostentation.

These are the principal scenes on one side of the gardens; on the other, close to the lawn before the house, is the winding valley above-mentioned; the lower part of it is assigned to the Elysian fields; they are watered by a lovely rivulet; are very lightsome, and very airy, so thinly are the trees scattered about them; are open at one end to more water and a larger glade; and the rest of the boundary is frequently broken to let in objects afar off, which appear still more distant from the manner of shewing them. The entrance is under a Doric arch, which co-incides with an opening among the trees, and forms a kind of vista, through which a Pembroke bridge just below, and a lodge built like a castle in the park, are seen in a beautiful perspective: that bridge is at one extremity of the gardens; the queen's pillar is at another; yet both are visible from the same station in the Elysian fields; and all these external objects are unaffectedly introduced, divested of their own appurtenances, and combined with others which belong to the spot: the temple of friendship also is in sight just without the place; and within it, are the temples of ancient virtue, and of the British worthies, the one in an elevated situation, the other low down in the valley, and near to the water: both are decorated with the effigies of those who have been most distinguished for military, civil, or literary merit; and near to the former stands a rostral column, sacred to the memory of captain Grenville, who fell in an action at sea: by placing here the meed of valour, and by filling these fields with the representations of those who have deserved best of mankind, the character intended to be given to the spot, is justly and poetically expressed; and the number of the images which are presented or excited, perfectly corresponds with it. Solitude was never reckoned among the charms of Elysium; it has been always pictured as the mansion of delight and of joy; and in this imitation, every circumstance accords with that established idea; the vivacity of the stream which flows through the vale; the glimpses of another approaching to join it; the sprightly verdure of the green-swerd, and every bust of the British worthies, reflected in the water; the variety of the trees; the lightness of their greens; their disposition; all of them distinct objects, and dispersed over gentle inequalities of the ground; together with the multiplicity of objects both within and without, which embellish and enliven the scene; give it a gaiety, which the imagination can hardly conceive, or the heart wish to be exceeded.

Close by this spot, and a perfect contrast to it, is the alder grove, a deep recess, in the midst of a shade, which the blaze of noon cannot brighten: the water seems to be a stagnated pool, eating into its banks, and of a peculiar colour, not dirty but clouded, and dimly reflecting the dun hue of the horse-chesnuts and alders, which press upon the brink; the stems of the latter, rising in clusters from the same root, bear one another down, and slant over the water: mishaped elms, and ragged firs are frequent in the wood which encompasses the hollow; the trunks of dead trees are left standing amongst them; and the uncouth sumach, and the yew, with elder, nut, and holly, compose the underwood; some limes and laurels are intermixt; but they are not many; the wood is in general of the darkest greens; and the foliage is thickened with ivy, which not only twines up the trees, but creeps also over the falls of the ground; they are steep and abrupt; the gravel walk is covered with moss; and a grotto at the end, faced with broken flints and pebbles, preserves in the simplicity of its materials, and the duskiness of its colour, all the character of its situation: two little rotundas near it were better away; one building is sufficient for such a scene of solitude as this, in which more circumstances of gloom concur than were ever perhaps collected together.

Immediately above the alder grove is the principal eminence in the gardens; it is divided by a great dip into two pinnacles, upon one of which is a large Gothic building; the space before this structure is an extensive lawn; the ground on one side falls immediately into the dip; and the trees which border the lawn, sinking with the ground, the house rises above them, and fills the interval: the vast pile seems to be still larger than it is; for it is thrown into perspective, and between and above the heads of the trees, the upper story, the porticoes, the turrets, and balustrades, and all the slated roofs appear in a noble confusion: on the other side of the Gothic building, the ground slopes down a long continued declivity into a bottom, which seems to be perfectly irriguous; divers streams wander about it in several directions; the conflux of that which runs from the Elysian fields with another below it, is full in sight; and a plain wooden bridge thrown over the latter, and evidently designed for a passage, imposes an air of reality on the river; beyond it is one of the Doric porticoes which front the house; but now it is alone; it stands on a little bank above the water, and is seen under some trees at a distance before it; thus grouped, and thus accompanied, it is a happy incident, concurring with many other circumstances to distinguish this landskip by a character of chearfulness and amenity.

From the Gothic building a broad walk leads to the Grecian valley, which is a scene of more grandeur than any in the gardens; it enters them from the park, spreading at first to a considerable breadth; then winds; grows narrower but deeper; and loses itself at last in a thicket, behind some lofty elms, which interrupt the sight of the termination: lovely woods and groves

hang all the way on the declivities; and the open space is broken by detached trees, which near the park are cautiously and
sparingly introduced, lest the breadth should be contracted by
them; but as the valley sinks, they advance more boldly down
the sides, stretch across or along the bottom, and cluster at
times into groupes and forms, which multiply the varieties of
the larger plantations: those are sometimes close coverts, and
sometimes open groves; the trees rise in one upon high stems,
and feather down to the bottom in another; and between them
are short openings into the park or the gardens. In the midst of
the scene, just at the bend of the valley, and commanding it on
both sides, upon a large, easy, natural rise, is placed the temple
of concord and victory: at one place its majestic front of six
Ionic columns, supporting a pediment filled with bas relief, and
the points of it crowned with statues, faces the view; at another,
the beautiful colonade on the side of ten lofty pillars, retires in
perspective; it is seen from every part, and impressing its own
character of dignity on all around, it spreads an awe over the
whole; but no gloom, no melancholy attends it; the sensations
it excites are rather placid; but full of respect, admiration, and
solemnity; no water appears to enliven, no distant prospect to
enrich the view; the parts of the scene are large; the idea of it
sublime; and the execution happy; it is independant of all adventitious circumstances; and relies on itself for its greatness.

The scenes which have been described are such as are most
remarkable for beauty or character; but the gardens contain many
more; and even the objects in these, by their several combinations,
produce very different effects, within the distance sometimes of a
few paces, from the unevenness of the ground, the variety of the
plantations, and the number of the buildings; the multiplicity of
the last has indeed been often urged as an objection to Stowe; and
certainly when all are seen by a stranger in two or three hours,
twenty or thirty capital structures, mixed with others of inferior
note, do seem too many; but the growth of the wood every day

weakens the objection, by concealing them one from the other; each belongs to a distinct scene; and if they are considered separately, at different times, and at leisure, it may be difficult to determine which to take away: yet still it must be acknowledged that their frequency destroys all ideas of silence and retirement: magnificence and splendor are the characteristics of Stowe; it is like one of those places celebrated in antiquity, which were devoted to the purposes of religion, and filled with sacred groves, hallowed fountains, and temples dedicated to several deities; the resort of distant nations; and the object of veneration to half the heathen world: this pomp is at Stowe blended with beauty; and the place is equally distinguished by its amenity and its grandeur.

In the midst of so much embellishment as may be introduced into this species of garden, a plain field, or a sheep walk, is sometimes an agreable relief; and even wilder scenes may occasionally be admitted: these indeed are not properly parts of a garden; but they may be comprehended within the verge of it; and their proximity to the more ornamented scenes is at least a convenience, that the transition from the one to the other may be easy, and the change always in our option; for though a spot in the highest state of improvement be a necessary appendage to a seat, yet in a place which is perfect, other characters will not be wanting; if they cannot be had on a large scale, they are acceptable on a smaller; and so many circumstances are common to all, that they may often be intermixt; they may always border on each other.

## Of a RIDING.

### LX.

Even a *Riding*, which in extent differs so widely from a garden, yet agrees with it in many particulars; for, exclusive of that community of character which results from their being both improvements, and both destined to pleasure, a closer relation arises from the property of a riding, *to extend the idea of a seat*, and appropriate a whole country to the mansion; for which purpose it must be distinguished from common roads; and the marks of distinction must be borrowed from a garden; those which a farm or a park can supply are faint and few; but whenever circumstances belonging to a garden occur, they are immediately received as evidence of the domaine; the *species* of the trees will often be decisive; plantations of firs, whether placed on the sides of the way, or in clumps or woods in the view, denote the neighbourhood of a seat; even limes and horse-chesnuts are not indifferent; for they have always been frequent in improvements, and rare in the ordinary scenes of cultivated nature: if the riding be carried through a wood, the shrubs, which for their beauty or their fragrance, have been transplanted from the country into gardens, such as the sweet-briar, the viburnum, the euonymus, and the wood-bine, should be encouraged in the underwood; and to these may be added several which are still peculiar to shruberies, but which might easily be transferred to the wildest coverts, and would require no further care.

Where the species are not, the *disposition* may be particular; and any appearance of *design* is a mark of improvement; a few trees standing out from a hedge-row, raise it to an elegance above common rusticity; and still more may be done by clumps in a field; they give it the air of a park: a close lane may be decorated with plantations in all the little vacant spaces: and even the groupes originally on the spot, (whether it be a wood, a field, or a lane,) if properly selected, and those only left which are elegant, will have an effect; though every beauty of this kind may be found in nature, yet many of them are seldom seen together, and never unmixed. The number and the choice are symptoms of design.

Another symptom is *variety*: if the appendages of the riding be different in different fields; if in a lane, or a wood, some distinguishing circumstance be provided for every bend; or, when carried over an open exposure, it winds to several points of view; if this be the conduct throughout, the intention is evident, to amuse the length of the way: variety of ground also is characteristic of a riding, when it seems to have proceeded from choice; and pleasure being the pursuit, the changes of the scene both compensate and account for the circuity.

But a part undistinguished from a common road, succeeding to others more adorned, will by the contrast alone be sometimes agreable; and there are beauties frequent in the high-way, and almost peculiar to it, which may be very acceptable in a riding: a green lane is always delightful; a passage winding between thickets of brambles and briars, sometimes with, sometimes without a little spring-wood rising amongst them, or a cut in a continued sweep through the furze of a down, or the fern of a heath, is generally pleasant. Nor will the character be absolutely lost in the interruption; it will soon be resumed; and never forgotten: when it has been once strongly impressed, very slight means will preserve the idea.

Simplicity may prevail the whole length of the way, when the way is all naturally pleasant; but especially if it be a communication between several spots, which in character are raised above the rest of the country: a fine open grove is unusual, except in a park or a garden; it has an elegance in the disposition which cannot be attributed to accident; and it seems to require a degree of preservation beyond the care of mere husbandry: a neat railing on the edge of a steep which commands a prospect, alone distinguishes that from other points of view: a building is still more strongly characteristic; it may be only ornamental; or it may be accommodated to the reception of company; for though a place to alight at interrupts the range of a riding; yet, as the object of an airing, it may often be acceptable; a small spot, which may be kept by the labour of one man, enclosed from the fields, and converted into a shrubery, or any other scene of a garden, will sometimes be a pleasing end to a short excursion from home; nothing so effectually extends the idea of a seat to a distance; and not being constantly visited it will always retain the charms of novelty and variety.

## LXI.

When a riding is carried along a high road, a kind of property may in appearance be claimed even there, by planting on both sides trees equidistant from each other, to give it the air of an approach; *regularity* intimates the neighbourhood of a mansion; a *village* therefore seems to be within the domaine, if any of the inlets to it are avenues; other formal plantations about it, and still more trivial circumstances, when they are evidently ornamental, sometimes produce, and always corroborate such an effect; but even without raising this idea, if the village be remarkable for its beauty, or only for its singularity, a passage through it may be an agreable incident in a riding.

The same ground which in the fields is no more than rough, often seems to be romantic, when it is the site of a village; the buildings and other circumstances mark and aggravate the irregularity: to strengthen this appearance, one cottage may be placed on the edge of a steep, and some winding steps of unhewn stone lead up to the door; another in a hollow, with all its little appurtenances hanging above it. The position of a few trees will sometimes answer the same purpose: a foot-bridge here and there for a communication between the sides of a narrow dip, will add to the character; and if there be any rills, they may be conducted so as greatly to improve it.

A village which has not these advantages of ground, may, however, be beautiful: it is distinguished by its elegance, when the larger intervals between the houses are filled with open groves, and little clumps are introduced upon other occasions.

The church often is, it generally may be made a picturesque object. Even the cottages may be neat, and sometimes grouped with thickets. If the place be watered by a stream, the crossings may be in a variety of pleasing designs; and if a spring rise, or only a well for common use be sunk, by the side of the way, a little covering over it may be contrived, which shall at the same time be simple and pretty.

There are few villages which may not easily be rendered agreable; a small alteration in a house will sometimes occasion a great difference in the appearance. By the help of a few trifling plantations, the objects which have a good effect may be shewn to advantage; those which have not may be concealed; and such as are similar be disguised. And any form which offends the eye, whether of ground, of trees, or of buildings, may sometimes be broken by the slightest circumstances, by an advanced paling, or only by a bench. Variety and beauty, in such a subject, are rather the effects of attention than expence.

## LXII.

But if the passage through the village cannot be pleasant; if the buildings are all alike, or stand in unmeaning rows and similar situations; if the place furnishes no opportunities to contrast the forms of dwellings with those of outhouses; to introduce trees and thickets; to interpose fields and meadows; to mix farms with cottages; and to place the several objects in different positions; yet on the *outside* even of such a village, there certainly is room for wood; and by that alone, the whole may be grouped into a mass, which shall be agreable when skirted by a riding; and still more so when seen from a distance. The separate farms in the fields also, by planting some trees about them, or perhaps only by managing those already on the spot, may be made very interesting objects; or if a new one is to be built, beauty may be consulted in the form of the house, and the disposition of its appurtenances. Sometimes a character not their own, as the semblance of a castle or an abbey, may be given to them; they will thereby acquire a degree of consideration, which they cannot otherwise be entitled to; and objects to improve the views are so important to a riding, that buildings must sometimes be erected for that purpose only; but they should be such as by an actual effect adorn or dignify the scene; not those little slight deceptions which are too well known to succeed, and have no merit if they fail: for though a fallacy sometimes contributes to support a character, or suggests ideas to the imagination; yet in itself it may be no improvement of a scene; and a bit of a turret, the tip of a spire, and the other ordinary subjects of these frivolous attempts, are so insignificant as objects, that whether they are real or fictitious is almost a matter of indifference.

## LXIII.

The same means by which the prospects from a riding are improved, may be applied to those from a garden; though they are not essential to its character, they are important to its beauty; and wherever they abound, the extent only of the range which commands them, determines whether they shall be seen from a riding or a garden. If they belong to the latter, that assumes in some degree the predominant properties of the former, and *the two characters approach very near to each other*: but still each has its peculiarities; progress is a prevailing idea in a riding; and the pleasantness of the way is, therefore, a principal consideration; but particular spots are more attended to in a garden; and to them the communications ought to be subordinate; their direction must be generally accommodated, their beauties sometimes sacrificed to the situation and the character of the scenes they lead to: an advantageous approach to these must be preferred to an agreable line for the *walk*; and the circumstances which might otherwise become it are misplaced, if they anticipate the openings; it should sometimes be contrasted to them; be retired and dark if they are splendid or gay, and simple if they are richly adorned. At other times it may burst unexpectedly out upon them; not on account of the surprize, which can have its effect only once; but the impressions are stronger by being sudden; and the contrast is enforced by the quickness of the transition.

In a riding the scenes are only the amusements of the way, through which it proceeds without stopping; in a garden they are principal; and the subordination of the walk raises their importance; every art, therefore, should be exerted to make them seem parts of the place; distant prospects cannot be so; and the alienation does not offend us; we are familiarized to it; the extent forbids every thought of a closer connexion; and if a continuation be preserved between them and the points which command them, we are satisfied; but *home-views* suggest other ideas; they appear to be within our reach; they are not only beautiful in prospect, but we can perceive that the spots are delightful; and we wish to examine, to inhabit and to enjoy them. Every apparent impediment to that gratification is a disappointment; and when the scenes begin beyond the opening, the consequence of the place is lowered; nothing within it engages our notice; it is an exhibition only of beauties, the property of which does not belong to it; and that idea, though indifferent in a riding, which is but a passage, is very disadvantageous to such a residence as a garden; to obviate such an idea the points of view should be made important; the objects within be appendages to those without; the separations be removed or concealed; and large portions of the garden be annexed to the spots which are contiguous to it. The ideal boundary of the place is then carried beyond the scenes which are thus appropriated to it; and the wide circuit in which they lie, the different positions in which they may be shewn, afford a greater variety than can generally be found in any garden, the scenery of which is confined to the enclosure.

*Persfield is not a large place; the park contains about three hundred acres; and the house stands in the midst of it. On the side of the approach, the inequalities of the ground are gentle, and the plantations pretty; but nothing there is great: on the other side a beautiful lawn falls precipitately every way into a deep vale which shelves down the middle; the declivities are diversified with clumps and with groves; and a number of large trees straggle along the bottom. This lawn is encompassed with wood; and through the wood are walks, which open beyond it upon those romantic scenes which surround the park, and which are the glory of Persfield. The Wye runs immediately below the wood; the river is of a dirty colour; but the shape of its course is very various, winding first in the form of a horse-shoe, then proceeding in a large sweep to the town of Chepstowe, and afterwards to the Severn. The banks are high hills; in different places steep, bulging out, or hollow on the sides; rounded, flattened, or irregular at top; and covered with wood, or broken by rocks. They are sometimes seen in front; sometimes in perspective; falling back from the passage, or closing behind the bend of the river; appearing to meet, rising above, or shooting out beyond one another. The wood which encloses the lawn crowns an extensive range of these hills, which overlook all those on the opposite shore, with the country which appears above or between them; and winding themselves as the river winds, their sides, all rich and beautiful, are alternately exhibited; and the point of view in one spot becomes an object to the next.

In many places the principal feature is a continued rock, in length a quarter of a mile, perpendicular, high, and placed upon a height: to resemble ruins is common to rocks; but no ruin of any single structure was ever equal to this enormous

* The seat of Mr. Morris, near Chepstowe, in Monmouthshire.

pile; it seems to be the remains of a city; and other smaller heaps scattered about it, appear to be fainter traces of the former extent, and strengthen the similitude. It stretches along the brow which terminates the forest of Dean; the face of it is composed of immense blocks of stone, but not rugged; the top is bare and uneven, but not craggy; and from the foot of it, a declivity, covered with thicket, slopes gently towards the Wye, but in one part is abruptly broken off by a ledge of less rocks, of a different hue, and in a different direction. From the grotto it seems to rise immediately over a thick wood, which extends down a hill below the point of view, across the valley through which the Wye flows, and up the opposite banks, hides the river, and continues without interruption to the bottom of the rock; from another seat it is seen by itself without even its base; it faces another, with all its appendages about it; and sometimes the sight of it is partially intercepted by trees, beyond which, at a distance, its long line continues on through all the openings between them.

Another capital object is the castle of Chepstowe, a noble ruin of great extent; advanced to the very edge of a perpendicular rock, and so immediately rivetted into it, that from the top of the battlements down to the river seems but one precipice: the same ivy which overspreads the face of the one, twines and clusters among the fragments of the other; many towers, much of the walls, and large remains of the chapel are standing. Close to it is a most romantic wooden bridge, very antient, very grotesque, at an extraordinary height above the river, and seeming to abut against the ruins at one end, and some rocky hills at the other. The castle is so near to the alcove at Persfield, that little circumstances in it may be discerned; from other spots more distant, even from the lawn, and from a shrubery on the side of the lawn, it is distinctly visible, and always beautiful, whether it is seen alone, or with the bridge, with the town, with more or with less of the rich meadows which lie along the banks of

the Wye, to its junction three miles off with the Severn. A long
sweep of that river also, its red cliffs, and the fine rising country
in the counties of Somerset, and Gloucester, generally terminate
the prospect.

Most of the hills about Persfield are full of rocks; some are
intermixed with hanging woods, and either advance a little before them, or retire within them, and are backed, or overhung,
or separated by trees. In the walk to the cave a long succession
of them is frequently seen in perspective, all of a dark colour,
and with wood in the intervals between them. In other parts the
rocks are more wild and uncouth; and sometimes they stand on
the tops of the highest hills; at other times down as low as the
river; they are home objects in one spot; and appear only in the
back-ground of another.

The woods concur with the rocks to render the scenes of
Persfield romantic; the place every where abounds with them;
they cover the tops of the hills; they hang on the steeps; or
they fill the depths of the vallies. In one place they front, in
another they rise above, in another they sink below the point
of view: they are seen sometimes retiring beyond each other,
and darkening as they recede; and sometimes an opening between two is closed by a third at a distance beyond them. A
point, called the Lover's Leap, commands a continued surface
of the thickest foliage, which overspreads a vast hollow immediately underneath. Below the Chinese seat the course of the
Wye is in the shape of a horse-shoe; it is on one side enclosed
by a semi-circular hanging wood; the direct steeps of a table-
hill shut it in on the other; and the great rock fills the interval
between them: in the midst of this rude scene lies the peninsula formed by the river, a mile at the least in length, and in
the highest state of cultivation: near the isthmus the ground
rises considerably, and thence descends in a broken surface, till
it flattens to the water's edge at the other extremity. The whole
is divided into corn-fields and pastures; they are separated by

hedge-rows, coppices, and thickets; open clumps and single trees stand out in the meadows; and houses and other buildings, which belong to the farms, are scattered amongst them: nature so cultivated, surrounded by nature so wild, compose a most lovely landskip together.

The communications between these several points are generally by close walks; but the covert ends near the Chinese seat; and a path is afterwards conducted through the upper park to a rustic temple, which over-looks on one side some of the romantic views which have been described, and on the other the cultivated hills and rich valleys of Monmouthshire. To the rude and magnificent scenes of nature now succeeds a pleasant, fertile, and beautiful country, divided into enclosures, not covered with woods, nor broken by rocks and precipices, but only varied by easy swells and gentle declivities; yet the prospect is not tame; the hills in it are high; and it is bounded by a vast sweep of the Severn, which is here visible for many miles together, and receives in its course the Wye and the Avon.

From the temple a road leads to the Windcliff, an eminence much above the rest, and commanding the whole in one view. The Wye runs at the foot of the hill; the peninsula lies just below; the deep bosom of the semi-circular hanging wood is full in sight: over part of it the great rock appears; all its base, all its accompaniments are seen; the country immediately beyond it is full of lovely hillocks; and the higher grounds in the counties of Somerset and Gloucester rise in the horizon. The Severn seems to be, as it really is, above Chepstowe, three or four miles wide; below the town it spreads almost to a sea; the county of Monmouth is there the hither shore; and between its beautiful hills appear at a great distance the mountains of Brecknock and Glamorganshire. In extent, in variety, and grandeur, few prospects are equal to this. It comprehends all the noble scenes of Persfield, encompassed by some of the finest country in Britain.

## Of the SEASONS.

### LXIV.

To every view belongs a light which shews it to advantage; every scene and every object is in its highest beauty only at particular hours of the day; and every place is, by its situation or its character, peculiarly agreable in certain months of the year. The *seasons* thus become subjects of consideration in gardening; and when several of those circumstances which distinguish a spot more at one time than another happen to concur, it will often be worth the while to add to their number, and to exclude such as do not agree with them, for no other purpose than to strengthen their effect at that particular time. Different parts may thus be adapted to different seasons; and each in its turn will be in perfection. But if the place will not allow of such a succession, still *occasional effects* may often be secured and improved without prejudice to the scene when they are past, and without affectation while they continue.

The temple of concord and victory at Stowe has been mentioned as one of the noblest objects that ever adorned a garden; but there is a moment when it appears in singular beauty; the setting sun shines on the long colonade which faces the west; all the lower parts of the building are darkened by the neighbouring wood; the pillars rise at different heights out of the obscurity; some of them are nearly overspread with it; some are chequered with a variety of tints; and others are illuminated almost down to their bases. The light is gently softened off by the rotundity of the columns; but it spreads in broad gleams upon the wall within them; and pours full and without interruption on all the entablature, distinctly marking every dentil: on the statues which adorn the several points of the pediment, a deep shade is contrasted to splendor; the rays of the sun linger on the side of the temple long after the front is over-cast with the sober hue of evening; and they tip the upper branches of the trees, or glow in the openings between them, while the shadows lengthen across the Grecian valley.

Such an occasional effect, however transient, is so exquisitely beautiful, that it would be unpardonable to neglect it. Others may be produced at several hours of the day; and the disposition of the buildings, of the ground, the water, and the plantations may often be accommodated to support them. There are also occasional effects in certain months or only weeks of the year, arising from some particular bloom, some occupation then carrying on, or other incident, which may so far deserve attention as to recommend a choice and arrangement of objects, which at that time will improve the composition, though at another they may have no extraordinary merit.

## LXV.

Besides these transitory effects, there are others which may be defined and produced with more exactness, which are fixed to stated periods, and have certain properties belonging to them. Some species and situations of objects are in themselves adapted to receive or to make the impressions which characterize the principal parts of the day; their splendor, their sobriety, and other peculiarities recommend or prohibit them upon different occasions; the same considerations direct the choice also of their appendages; and in consequence of a judicious assemblage and arrangement of such as are proper for the purpose, the *spirit* of the morning, the *excess* of noon, or the *temperance* of evening, may be improved or corrected by the application of the scene to the season.

In a *morning*, the freshness of the air allays the force of the sunbeams, and their brightness is free from glare; the most splendid objects do not offend the eye; nor suggest the idea of heat in its extreme; but they correspond with the glitter of the dew which bespangles all the produce of the earth, and with the chearfulness diffused over the whole face of the creation. A variety of buildings may therefore be introduced to enliven the view; their colour may be the purest white, without danger of excess, though they face the eastern sun; and those which are in other aspects should be so contrived, that their turrets, their pinnacles, or other points, may catch glances of the rays, and contribute to illuminate the scene. The trees ought in general to be of the lightest greens, and so situated as not to darken much of the landskip by the length of their shadows. Vivacity in the streams, and transparency in a lake, are more important at this than at any other hour of the day; and an open exposure is commonly the most delightful, both for the effect of particular objects, and the general character of the scene.

At *noon* every expedient should be used to correct the excess of the season: the shades are shortened; they must therefore be thick; but open plantations are generally preferable to a close covert; they afford a passage, or at least admittance to the air, which tempered by the coolness of the place, soft to the touch, and refreshing at once to all the senses, renders the shade a delightful climate, not a mere refuge from heat. Groves, even at a distance, suggest the ideas which they realize on the spot; and by multiplying the appearances, improve the sensations of relief from the extremity of the weather: grottos, caves, and cells, are on the same account agreable circumstances in a sequestered recess; and though the chill within be hardly ever tolerable, the eye catches only an idea of coolness from the sight of them. Other buildings ought in general to be cast into shade, that the glare of the reflection from them may be obscured. The large expanse of a lake, is also too dazzling; but a broad river moving gently, and partially darkened with shadow, is very refreshing; more so perhaps than a little rill; for the vivacity of the latter rather disturbs the repose which generally prevails at mid-day: every breeze then is still; the reflexion of an aspin leaf scarcely trembles on the water; the animals remit their search of food; and man ceases from his labour;

the steam of heat seems to oppress all the faculties of the mind, and all the active powers of the body; and any very lively motion discomposes the languor in which we then delight to indulge. To hear, therefore, the murmurs of a brook purling underneath a thicket, or the echo of falling waters through a wood, is more agreable than the sight of a current; the idea conveyed by the sound is free from any agitation; but if no other stream than a rill can be introduced, the refreshment which attends the appearance of water must not be denied to the scene.

In the *evening* all splendor fades; no buildings glare; no water dazzles; the calmness of a lake suits the quiet of the time; the light hovers there, and prolongs the duration of day. An open reach of a river has a similar, though a fainter effect; and a continued stream all exposed, preserves the last rays of the sun along the whole length of its course, to beautify the landskip. But a brisk current is not so consistent as a lake with the tranquillity of evening; and other objects should in general conform to the temper of the time; buildings of a dusky hue are most agreable to it; but a very particular effect from a setting sun will recommend those of a brighter colour; and they may also be sometimes used, among other means, to correct the uniformity of twilight. No contrast of light and shade can then be produced; but if the plantations which by their situation are the first to be obscured, be of the darkest greens; if the buildings which have a western aspect be of a light colour; and if the management of the lawns and the water be adapted to the same purpose, a diversity of tints will be preserved long after the greater effects are faded.

## LXVI.

The delights, however, of the morning and evening are confined to a few months of the year; at other times two or three hours before, and as much after noon, are all that are pleasant; and even then the heat is seldom so extreme as to require relief from its excess. The distinctions therefore between the three parts of the day may in general be reckoned among the characteristics of summer; the occasional effects which by the position of objects may occur at any hour, are common to all the seasons of the year; and such as arise from the accidental colours of plants, though they are more frequent and more beautiful in one season than another, yet exist in all: and very agreable groupes may be formed by an assemblage of them. A degree of importance may be given even to the flowers of a border, if instead of being indiscriminately mixed, they are arranged according to their heights, their sizes, and their colours, so as to display their beauties, and to blend or contrast their varieties to the greatest advantage. The bloom of shrubs differs from that of flowers only in the scale; and the tints occasioned by the hue of the berry, the foliage, or the bark, are sometimes little inferior to bloom. By collecting into one spot such plants as have at the same time their accidental colours, considerable effects may be produced from the concurrence of many little causes.

Those which arise from bloom are the most striking, and the most certain; and they abound chiefly in the *spring*; bloom is a characteristic of the season; and a villa near town, which is designed principally for that time of the year, is not adapted to its use, if this property be not amply provided for. In such a place, therefore, shrubberies, with an intermixture of flowers, are peculiarly proper. In the summer months, a border between the thicket and the greensword, breaks the connexion, and destroys the greater effect; it ought not to be then introduced, except to enliven small spots, and as the best species of parterre. But in the spring, the thicket is hardly formed; its principal beauty is bloom; and flowers before or among the shrubs, are agreable to the character of the season. An orchard, which at other times is unsightly, is then delightful; and if a farm joins to the garden, should not be forgotten: but evergreens appear in general to great disadvantage; most of them have a russet or a dark hue, which suffers by being contrasted to the lively verdure of the young shoots on the deciduous trees; that verdure is, however, so light, and so universal, that effects from a mixture of greens can seldom be produced; and those which depend on a depth of shade will often be disappointed; but buildings, views of water, and whatever tends to animate the scene, accord with the season, which is full of youth and vigour, fresh and sprightly, brightened by the verdure of the herbage and the woods, gay with blossoms and flowers, and enlivened by the songs of the birds in all their variety, from the rude joy of the sky lark, to the delicacy of the nightingale.

In *summer* both the buildings and the water are agreable, not as objects only, but also as circumstances of refreshment; the pleasantness, therefore, of the rooms in the former, of the seats and the walks near the latter, is to be regarded. The plantations also should be calculated at least as much for places of retreat, as for ornaments of the view; and a continuation of shade be preserved, with very few and short interruptions, through all the parts of the garden. Communications by gravel walks are of less consequence; they do not suggest that idea of utility which attends them in winter or autumn; and their colour which in spring is a lively contrast to the verdure through which it winds, is in the intemperate blaze of a summer day, glaring and painful. They should, therefore, be concealed as much as possible; and the other considerations which belong to the noon-tide hour, should be particularly attended to; at the same time that the delights of the morning and the evening are also liberally provided for. But exclusive of all such incidental circumstances, the scenes of nature in general appear at this season to the greatest advantage; though the bloom of the spring be faded, and the verdure of the herbage may be sometimes affected by drought; yet the richness of the produce of the earth, and the luxuriance of the foliage in the woods, the sensations of refreshment added to the beauty of water, the ideas of enjoyment which accompany the sight of every grove, of every building, and every delightful spot; the characters of rocks, heightened by their appendages, and unallayed by any disconsolate reflections; the connexion of the ground with the plantations; the permanency of every tint; and the certainty of every effect; all concur in summer to raise the several compositions to their highest state of perfection.

But maturity is always immediately succeeded by decay; flowers bloom and fade; fruits ripen and rot; the grass springs and withers; and the foliage of the woods shoots, thickens, and falls. In the latter months of *autumn*, all nature is on the decline; it is a comfortless season; not a blossom is left on the shrubs or the trees; and the few flowers which still remain in the borders, dripping with wet, and sickening even as they blow, seem hardly to survive the leaves of the plant which are shrivelling beneath them; but the change of the leaf precedes the fall; and thence results a variety of colours superior to any which the spring or the summer can boast of. To shew and to improve that variety should be principally attended to, in a place, such as a sporting seat, which is frequented only in autumn. It appears to advantage, whenever the surface of a wood can be commanded; and it may be produced to a considerable degree even in a shrubbery, if the plants are so disposed as to rise in gradation one behind another. By observing the tints which the leaves assume when they change, the choice may be directed to the improvement of their variety; and by attending to the times when they fall, a succession of these transitory beauties may be provided, from the earliest to the latest in the season. Many shrubs and trees are at this time also covered with berries, which furnish still further varieties of colour; both evergreens and deciduous plants abound with them; and the verdure of the former is besides a welcome substitute to that which is daily fading away. Open buildings, airy groves, views of water, and the other delights of summer, now lose their charms; and more homely circumstances of comfort and convenience are preferable to all their beauties.

A place which is the residence of a family all the year is very defective, if some portion of it be not set apart for the enjoyment of a fine day, for air and exercise in *winter*: to such a spot shelter is absolutely essential; and evergreens being the thickest covert, are therefore the best; their verdure also is then agreable to the eye; and they may be arranged so as to produce beautiful mixtures of greens, with more certainty than deciduous trees, and with almost equal variety: they may be collected into a wood, and through that wood gravel walks may be led, along openings of a considerable breadth, free from large trees, which would intercept the rays of the sun, and winding in such a manner as to avoid any draft of wind, from whatever quarter it may blow. But when a retreat at all times is thus secured, other spots may be adapted only to occasional purposes; and be sheltered towards the north or the east on one hand, while they are open to the sun on the other: the few hours of chearfulness, and warmth which its beams afford are so valuable, as to justify the sacrifice even of the principles of beauty, to the enjoyment of them; and therefore no objections of sameness or formality, can prevail against the pleasantness of a straight walk, under a thick hedge, or a south wall: the eye may however be diverted from the skreen, by a border before it, where the aconite and the snowdrop, the crocus and hepatica, brought forward by the warmth of the situation, will be welcome harbingers of spring; and on the opposite side of the walk, little tufts of laurustines, and of variegated evergreens, may be planted. The spot thus enlivened by a variety of colours, and even a degree of bloom, may be still further improved by a green-house; the entertainment which exotics afford peculiarly belongs to this part of the year; and if amongst them be interspersed some of our earliest flowers, they will there blow before their time, and anticipate the gaiety of the season which is advancing. The walk may also lead to the stoves, where the climate and the plants are always the same: and the kitchen garden should not be far off; for that is never quite destitute of produce, and always an active scene; the appearance of business is alone engaging; and the occupations there are an earnest of the happier seasons to which they are preparative. By these expedients even the winter may be rendered chearful in a place, where shelter is provided against all but the bitterest inclemencies of the sky, and agreable objects, and interesting amusements are contrived for every hour of tolerable weather.

# CONCLUSION.

## LXVII.

Whatever contributes to render the scenes of nature delightful, is amongst the subjects of gardening; and animate as well as inanimate objects, are circumstances of beauty or character. Several of these have been occasionally mentioned; others will readily occur; and nothing is unworthy of the attention of a gardener, which can tend to improve his compositions, whether by immediate effects, or by suggesting a train of pleasing ideas. The whole range of nature is open to him, from the parterre to the forest; and whatever is agreable to the senses or the imagination, he may appropriate to the spot he is to improve: it is a part of his business to collect into one place, the delights which are generally dispersed through different species of country.

But in this application, the genius of the place must always be particularly considered; to force it is hazardous; and an attempt to contradict it is always unsuccessful. The beauties peculiar to one character, cannot be transferred to its opposite; even where the characters are the same, it is difficult to copy directly from the one into the other; and by endeavouring to produce a resemblance of a scene which is justly admired, the proper advantages of the place, are often neglected for an imitation much inferior to the original. The excellence of the latter probably depends on the happy application of the circumstances to the subject; and the subjects of both are never exactly alike. The art of gardening therefore is not to be studied in those spots only where it has been exercised; though they are in this country very numerous, and very various: yet all together they contain but a small proportion of the beauties which nature exhibits; and unless the gardener has stored his mind with ideas, from the infinite variety of the country at large, he will feel the want of that number, which is necessary for choice; he will have none ready to apply to the subject immediately before him; and will be reduced to copy an imitation. But improved places are of singular use to direct the judgment in the choice, and the combinations of the beauties of nature: an extensive knowledge of them is to be acquired in the country where they casually occur; discernment of their excellencies, and a taste for the disposition of them, is to be formed in places where they have been selected, and arranged with design.

FINIS.

Figure 2. The 'conical hill': the flat-topped Thorpe Cloud, near Ilam, Staffordshire. Anonymous print c.1780.

Figure 3. Belvedere, house and grove planting at Esher Place, Surrey. Engraving by Thomas Medland after Meheux, 1792.

Three ill-shaped trees, formed into a good group.

[*Page* 241.

Figure 4. Three ill-shaped trees, formed into a pleasing group. From *Gilpin's Forest Scenery* (1883 edition of William Gilpin's original text of 1791), p. 239.

Figure 5. Brown's lake and Vanbrugh's bridge at Blenheim, Oxfordshire. Engraving by William Angus after Lord Duncannon, 1787 (published as Plate V in Angus's *The Seats of the Nobility and Gentry in Great Britain and Wales*).

Figure 6. View of cascade near Matlock Bath, Derbyshire. Engraved for *The Modern Universal British Traveller*, 1779.

Figure 7. The New Weir, Herefordshire, from the river. Aquatint by Jukes after William Gilpin, from Gilpin's *Observations on the River Wye...* (1770) (London: R. Blamire, 1789), 2nd edn, opposite p. 65.

Figure 8. View in Dovedale, Derbyshire. Engraving by E. Finden after W. Westall, 1829.

Figure 9. Humphry Repton's trade card. Engraving by Thomas Medland after Repton, 1788.

Figure 10. View of Tintern Abbey, Monmouthshire. Aquatint by Jukes after William Gilpin, from Gilpin's *Observations on the River Wye...* (1770) (London: R. Blamire, 1789), 2nd edn, opposite p. 45.

Figure II. Tintern Abbey as garden ruin. Print probably early nineteenth century.

Figure 12. General view of The Leasowes, West Midlands, including ruined priory and Virgil's Grove on left. Engraving by Benjamin Pouncy after Evans, 1792.

Figure 13. Vignette of Woburn Farm, Surrey. Engraving by G.F. Schroeder after C.F. Weiksteed, early nineteenth century.

Figure 14. West side of Grotto Island, Painshill, Surrey. Engraving by Wiliam Woollett, 1760.

Figure 15. Dense plantings at Hagley, Worcestershire. Engraving by François Vivares after Thomas Smith, 1749.

Figure 16. View of Temple of Venus, called Kent's Building by Whately, at Stowe, Buckinghamshire. Drawn and engraved by Thomas Medland, 1797.

Figure 17. View of the Wyndcliff from Piercefield, Monmouthshire. Engraving by J. Newman, 1842.

Figure 18. Temple of Concord and Victory at Stowe, Buckinghamshire. Drawn and engraved by Thomas Medland, 1797.

# LATAPIE AND WHATELY

François de Paule Latapie played a massive part in the promulgation of Whately through Europe. He was a botanist who learned from the philosopher Montesquieu at Labrède, where there may have been something of an English park. Montesquieu had been in England in 1729–30, immediately following Voltaire, and both men absorbed ideas of the English constitution to the extent of wishing to copy it in France. Latapie accompanied Montesquieu's son to Italy and came to England in 1770, visiting Stowe and Blenheim, among other places. He eventually held the Chair at the botanical Jardin des Plantes at Bordeaux.

## LATAPIE'S PREFACE

Latapie published his French edition of Whately, *L'Art de former les jardins modernes...ou L'Art des jardins anglois*, in 1771. There was an extended preface, which included a little garden history going back to the Assyrians and Greeks, leading to Le Nôtre as the apogee of the French garden. Latapie sought to demolish the originality of the English garden by claiming that the Frenchman Charles Dufresny had beaten William Kent to the first steps of the 'natural' look in gardens as early as the 1720s. He was clearly anxious to deny England the credit for introducing the landscape garden, and his manifestly French slant colours the book and therefore would tend to influence the reader. Whately himself had neither looked at garden history nor claimed originality for the landscape garden.

The preface continues with two lengthy quotations pressing the case for Chinese influence on the 'natural' garden. One is a chapter from William Chambers' book on Chinese design (1757) and the other an extract from Father Attiret's description of the royal palace gardens at Peking (Beijing) (1749). Their inclusion was clearly to demonstrate that China had already embraced the natural approach to garden design, which would contribute to the French concept of *le jardin anglo-chinois* (G.-L. Le Rouge copied Latapie a few years later in reproducing the same section from Chambers as the fifth *cahier* of his albums of prints of English and French gardens). There then follows the translation of a letter from Whately to Latapie dated December 1770, which is preceded by a foreword about Whately.

Latapie declares that the modestly titled *Observations* is the only known work on the subject of the English garden. He believes that, in addition to garden-lovers and designers, the book will appeal to people of taste, artists and, above all, painters for its thoughts on perspective and on art generally; to philosophers for valuable and sometimes profound reflections on the effects of being stirred by certain objects; and to poets for the vivid descriptions of the most beautiful English gardens of all kinds, all of which show the author to have an ever-observant eye, a great knowledge of the fine arts, a keen imagination and an instinct for thinking. Latapie does not conceal, however, that some people of sense (even among the English) reproach Whately for delving too deeply into reflections, subtle distinctions and metaphysics, rendering his style obscure. He states that Whately has not always clarified his ideas and principles by means of examples, nor used engravings; and that, in advocating the new style, he has banished formality too rigorously.

Latapie considers that the English are in general deeper thinkers than the French and often sacrifice grace of style for profundity. In addition, their turns of phrase are entirely in accordance with their unique way of seeing and feeling, and demand more attention and concentration than does listening to a lecture. As to other objections, Latapie records that he took the liberty of putting them to Whately, who had the courtesy to reply late in 1770. He hopes that Whately will not take it ill that he is left to defend himself through the present translation of his letter. The letter is not given in full, however, but contains 'the most interesting parts'.

## WHATELY'S LETTER

This is a translation back into English, so will not be identical to Whately's original, which is not known to have survived:

You would have wished, Monsieur, that my work had not been so concise and that to render it more intelligible I should have included engravings. To tell you the truth, I hadn't expected this slight essay would ever have aroused the curiosity of foreigners. Besides, you know that it is hardly possible that my observations and descriptions would be perfectly understood by those who have never visited England. My compatriots are so familiar with the modern art of gardens, and all the country seats I have described are so generally known, that I have not hesitated to indulge my taste for brevity.

Engravings would have been more useful for foreigners than for us English. I would wish, however, with all my heart to be able to satisfy you on this point: but I must say that I am very discriminating about all representations of nature, and I would rather have none at all than any which are second-rate. The most beautiful natural views are almost always of little interest in a picture. Besides, our gardens exhibit such numerous and varied scenes that one wouldn't know how to procure engravings, even mediocre ones, without a lot of trouble and expense. We do have some which are reasonably well produced technically, but apart from the fact that no taste is shown in the choice of views, the places have changed so much that prints can only represent them imperfectly. Even those of Stowe bear only a feeble resemblance to reality.

I have not mentioned a number of famous gardens celebrated for their beauty and singularity, but for the purposes of my descriptions I have chosen those which, under each category, were best known to me and which seemed most appropriate to the subject.

I readily confess that I am an enemy to symmetry and that no one admires more sincerely the new taste that reigns in the gardens of England – but regularity, you tell me, is one of the sources of beauty. Yes, when it is accompanied by utility. But it is not sufficient for it to be useful; when it replaces the freedom and variety of nature it has to be necessary. I believe I have explained this adequately in the section on Art. You have seen there that I tolerate regularity in certain circumstances, to which one can add *public gardens*, although I have not mentioned them because it wasn't part of my plan. Gardens of this kind form a class apart and must be designed according to different principles than private gardens. The object would be lost if avenues were not planted in very broad and straight lines. I believe, Monsieur, that these general remarks form a sufficient response to your question about the Tuileries. It is on the same principle that, in the section on Seasons, I have emphasised the need for a straight avenue to be covered with gravel for winter exercise. I have said that symmetry must reign in architecture, because that is an absolute necessity and on that the solidity and convenience of buildings depend.

How could symmetry be a source of beauty in our gardens,

218

seeing that it displeases us even in those circumstances which it seems to suit in a particular way? The two sides of the human body resemble each other: however, for a pose or posture to be pleasing, the limbs have to be in opposing or contrasting positions. Will you permit me this comparison? The ancient gardens are to the new as an Egyptian mummy is to a beautiful antique statue.

You will be very pleased, Monsieur, to learn what I think of the possibility of establishing gardens in the English taste in France. As I have never been there, I can't respond to this question in a precise way. I can't imagine, however, that France differs so greatly from England that it would be impossible to create gardens of the same sort (1). I acknowledge that the constant humidity of our climate produces that beautiful green growth for us which you must generally do without. But what should console you is that some of our most beautiful gardens benefit very little from this advantage because the soil composition is not favourable (2). Wouldn't you be able to profit in France from those situations where a conjunction of fortunate circumstances would compensate for the disadvantages of the climate by producing beautiful shades of green? Wouldn't it be possible for you (if you were to conduct some serious research) to discover some species of grass that would remain green longer than those you use now? It wouldn't be necessary for you to conserve lawns for ever in a state of perfection. That would be impossible for us too, since our gardens are now so much more extensive; and we are much less scrupulous on this point than formerly. We now plough many sections of land that we used to cover with turf. As to less extensive lawns, I can't imagine that it is particularly difficult in France to maintain a beautiful green grass if the ground is well watered. It is true that if one were to water only lightly, irregularly and at different times of day, the grass will soon perish, burned by the sun: but if on the contrary the waterings are always abundant (an effect one can achieve with machines), and if it is only done in the evening, so that the soil would be completely soaked before sunrise, I am convinced you would have most beautiful, and even very extensive, lawns without exorbitant expense.

(1) My only difficulty was with lawns: but for the rest, France is admirable for gardens of the natural kind. It is watered everywhere by superb rivers edged with very varied banks: high mountains cross the country, and it presents the most extensive and agreeable views in all parts.

(2) Sir William Temple has made the same remark; he adds that no sand can be found as attractive for avenues as that in England. I don't know if this is true.

It will be seen from the above that Whately's three main points, in answer to specific issues raised by Latapie, are the non-use of engravings; regularity in gardens (in singling out public gardens he surely has the London pleasure gardens such as Vauxhall, with its grid system, in mind); and the difficulties of producing English-style lawns abroad. He also explains his (limited) choice of gardens as examples. Together these points constitute an important addendum to, and gloss on, his book.

# THE *OBSERVATIONS*

The translated text of *Observations* contains notes and comments, and is followed by a description of Latapie's visit to Stowe, with a map. Commenting on his translation, Latapie said that he had been asked to expand some obscure points, that it was claimed that he had suppressed certain details and that it was said he was too inclined to improve on English style. He himself thought it would be better to translate the whole work just as it was, only rarely allowing himself to paraphrase or abridge.

The translation is generally close and faithful to the original. However, Latapie has difficulty with some of Whately's more technical terms, such as the sub-division of wood into clump, thicket and grove, which he says is peculiar to the author. He can find no exact French equivalent to 'riding', but thinks that 'carrière' comes closest to it. Also, in rendering 'gardener' as 'jardinier', he points out that the French term does not mean a garden designer, which Whately does. And when Whately moves into more theoretical territory, where he deals with scenes and their character, Latapie feels he has to borrow from 'moral and dramatic' language.

He says that his purpose in translating Whately was to convey to the French a coherent idea of gardens as they actually existed in England. He has a number of footnotes that show him to be far from uncritical. He takes issue with Whately over a number of points, some of which are dealt with in Whately's letter. A few notes are simply explanatory (identification of trees or explicating the 'Tinian lawn' at Hagley), but most express Latapie's own opinions. He finds Whately sometimes too metaphysical or too brief, which makes for obfuscation. He objects to Whately's dismissal of sculpture, understandably citing Versailles. Although he praises Whately for his emotional response to gardens, saying he has a fine and great imagination, like Plato, he queries his reaction to the temples at Stowe: 'The more I reflect on this passage, the less I am of the author's opinion.' He also queries Whately's belief that orchards are attractive only in spring, claiming that others find them so at other times, some trees keeping their leaves.

Occasionally Latapie has a dig at the English, as when he discusses Whately's description of the simple 'truckle' boats that plied at the New Weir: he thinks it curious that so advanced a civilisation should employ such primitive craft. He also defends the use of inscriptions in gardens (which

Whately tended to find tiresome), claiming that the English abused them.

Latapie does not hesitate to point out the differences between English and French gardens not only in the practical terms of climate and soil but also in perceptions and ways of thinking about gardens. He declares that English grass is beautiful, but it is always moist, unlike in France. The section on the seasons, says Latapie, relates entirely to the English climate. He also comments that foreigners cannot understand the differences between the English park and garden (a view not confined to foreigners, one might add). Other peculiarly English features include animated objects in the scene and traditional melancholy, seen as a contributory source of the Sublime.

In one of the notes Latapie cites his old mentor Montesquieu on taste. The latter, he says, declares that our soul finds pleasure when it has a feeling it cannot pin down and which is totally different to the norm.

Latapie considers Whately (last sentence of section LXII) to be indifferent as to whether one is convinced by an image or the reality: 'I swear I cannot reconcile this reflection either with the rules of logic or with the author's system.'


# DESCRIPTION OF STOWE

Latapie gives a long description of Stowe, which he had visited the previous year, that follows the *Observations*. He states that it is so famous in England and abroad and is a perfect example of *le jardin anglois* that he thinks readers would appreciate having a description. He claims Whately examined only the larger effects of view and prospect and neglected the details, so he will remedy that. His account will be a kind of commentary, which will serve to clarify certain of

Whately's observations that are unintelligible to those who haven't seen gardens in England.

This preamble instantly throws up problems and misunderstandings. First, while Stowe was indubitably the most celebrated of English gardens, it was by no means typical and by the second half of the century was even sometimes perceived as in questionable taste, with so many buildings. The qualities that marked the understanding and the success of the English garden abroad, principally naturalness, could be more eloquently conveyed by many other gardens. Second, as has already been discussed, Whately did not intend to provide detailed guidebook-style descriptions, and so can hardly be blamed for not doing so. Indeed, Latapie must surely have known that Stowe, of all places, had comprehensive guidebooks, which is one reason why Whately did not follow suit, and must have perused them for fleshing out some of his details. In particular it is likely that some if not all of the inscriptions (which Latapie gives in both the original language and French) were taken from guidebooks. He refrained, however, from translating the indelicate verses in St Augustine's Cave.

Overall, Latapie's account is full of enthusiasm, especially when it comes to the views, the lawns and the buildings. He found the cascade a brilliant imitation of the ancients, and declared it to be the most piquant and animated of all the scenes at Stowe. But he thought poorly of Vanbrugh and said that the whole of England was deceived in thinking him a distinguished architect. Blenheim, said Latapie, would be a monument to his bad taste. He had already criticised Vanbrugh's Blenheim in a note to the *Observations*, finding the bridge heavy and ungainly. Vanbrugh's Rotunda at Stowe was saved by having been 'perfected' by Borra in mid-century. But in general Latapie found that poetic ideas were stimulated by the imagination while traversing the gardens.

Not unexpectedly, Latapie disapproved of the Temple of Concord and Victory (though he considered it the most beautiful of the garden buildings), because of the medallions that celebrated victories of the English over the French in the Seven Years' War: it was too nationalistic. But he judged the Temple of British Worthies universally uplifting and described it as 'un spectacle délicieux'. He overlooked Brown's role in the gardens but saw Kent as the principal creator, possibly as a result of noting several key buildings by him.

In his description of the Grecian Valley Latapie records the presence of a number of sculptures among the trees. These had been arriving in the valley from the 1750s and would certainly have been seen by Whately, who fails, however, to mention them. Did Whately therefore deliberately suppress them in the interests of presenting the valley as more 'natural' than it actually was?

As a result of accessing Latapie's edition, accordingly, readers would get a full impression of Whately but seen and judged through French eyes. Anything perceived as anti-French is firmly quashed, and English attempts to claim credit for the landscape garden are likewise denied. But the principal virtue may be the practical one of discussing the differences between English and continental gardens, often resulting from climate, and the difficulties of implementing the landscape garden in France (and by extension Europe).

# COMMENTARY

## INTRODUCTION

Far from being a bland, explanatory foreword to the text, Whately's introduction is bold, assertive and in some respects novel. He has no hesitation in pushing landscape gardening to the fore, ahead of landscape painting, and in claiming that, as a result of imagination and taste, the best possible aspects and views of nature are now accessible through garden design. Nature is therefore seen as the heart of the landscape garden. Whately's division of garden, park, farm and riding is his own (to be queried by some): there could be less quarrel with his categorising of nature's four materials (ground, wood, water and rocks), though William Marshall subsequently excluded rocks as a separate material.[35] Buildings are then added, which confirms Whately's structured *modus operandi*. Walpole, while not criticising Whately's divisions, preferred to take a historical line which led him to three basic categories, the garden connecting with a park, the *ferme ornée* and the forest or savage garden, Painshill being the perfect example of the last.[36] Shenstone reduced landscape gardens to a single head, which he called 'landskip, or picturesque-gardening', while acknowledging that garden scenes 'may perhaps be divided into the sublime, the beautiful, and the melancholy or pensive'.[37] He, like Whately, based this on Burke.

# OF GROUND

Whately's approach is predominantly visual, with his emphasis on variety and contrast revealing an aesthetic in tune with the Picturesque. He is particularly concerned about making a flat area interesting to the eye, and illustrates this by showing how the owner of Moor Park, Hertfordshire, planted to break up the evenness of a vast lawn and added hillocks to 'convert a deformity into a beauty'. In this practical example Whately is in effect showing not just what a successful attempt looks like but how it was achieved.

What brings us up short is the sudden disparagement of the ha-ha, normally reckoned (by Walpole and others) to be the masterstroke in bringing the countryside into the garden. Many landscape gardens, especially Brown's, relied on the device to provide a seamless transition. But Whately has no time for what he calls a 'fosse' – that is, a sunken ditch or ha-ha. He asserts: 'To blend the garden with the country is no part of the idea: the cattle, the objects, the culture [cultivation], without [outside] the sunk fence, are discordant to all within, and keep up the division.' In other words, the ha-ha tends actually to call attention to the difference in character inside and outside the garden. Whately proposes, mainly through planting, disguising the fosse so that its line is obscured. Indeed, planting may be enough in itself, rather than having to move earth.

It is planting, too, that can rectify a hollow that appears no more than a hole, or a swell no more than a heap. In this way what nature appears to have left aesthetically deficient can be made good. But every piece of ground is distinguished by certain properties and has its own character.

The essence of Whately's argument is that all the parts of a scene should contribute to the overall effect, and that, furthermore, the style of each part should be appropriate to

226

the prevailing character of the whole. But unusual features can surprise and astonish, as witness the truncated conical hill (Thorp Cloud) at Ilam, Staffordshire (Fig. 2), which, among an irregular jumble of hills, 'rivets the attention'.

# OF WOOD

Whately has already paved the way for demonstrating the efficacy of plantings in adjusting the effects of the natural lie of the ground, but in this section he concentrates on the characteristic differences of trees and shrubs, though visual rather than botanical. Differences can be between types of branch or shades of green. The massed effect of colour is considerable – and can vary according to the season (e.g. autumnal changes to shades of red). Colours can also be manipulated in the interests of perspective: thus, a tree or clump of light green will seem to be further away than one of darker hue.

Whately divides plantations into wood, grove, clump or single tree. A grove consists of trees without an understorey and a clump may be subdivided into close (dense) and open, represented by thickets and groups of trees respectively. It is these distinctions that taxed Latapie's comprehension. Whately considers that each division has its own effect and impact: thus the predominant character of a substantial wood is grandeur, whereas that of a grove is beauty, since it is constituted of a collection of fine trees. The grouping or massing of trees can vary from unified to disjointed according to the shape of the land.

Groupings are illustrated by reference to Claremont, Surrey, which at the time of publication pre-dated Brown's arrival there. The variety and undulations of clumps and groups which Whately commends are the result of plantings by Kent and, after his death, by his assistant Stephen Wright, who formed the grotto and in whose time Bridgeman's enormous formal amphitheatre was planted over. But Whately evidently thinks it was all due to Kent.

Adjacent to Claremont, Esher Place 'was planted by the same masterly hand' (Fig. 3), although variety of effect was constrained by new plantations having to cede priority to large existing trees. Variety of situation, however, more than compensates (says Whately) for lack of variety in the arrangement of plantings. Nonetheless he does not hesitate to criticise Kent for planting trees too close together, saying that lessons have now been learned (in fact Kent is understood to have deliberately planted closely, with a view to weeding out the inferior specimens later). Light and shade are important considerations, the density and texture of the trees determining how much light is admitted.

There follows a lengthy disquisition on clumps, defined as small woods (if dense) or small groves (if open). A clump must comprise a minimum of two trees, though they should appear as one block. They can admit some underplanting as long as they do not straggle. Their functions are various: to be beautiful in themselves or to break up a lawn or a continued line. Whately has no time, however, for artificial hills to be thrown up in order to be crowned with a clump. The effect is contrived, as is having too many separate clumps. Single trees follow the same prescriptions, their best use being to provide variety or interest, together with their proportionate value in the scene as a whole. Any arrangement of trees, if not in a pattern, is sure to appear natural. Large existing trees can be 'finer' objects.

Gilpin, by contrast, in his *Remarks on Forest Scenery, and other Woodland Views* (1791, but written a decade earlier), concentrates on the aesthetics of more detailed appearances, such as the withered top of a tree or how individually misshapen trees can form a picturesque group (Fig. 4).

# OF WATER

Water, claims Whately, is the most interesting object in a landscape, and its absence is always regrettable (cf. Count Kielmansegge declaring in 1761, 'an Englishman thinks nothing of a garden without water').[38] It may produce an emotional effect or lead to contemplation, and can adopt various forms, running or standing, and sizes, from rill to river. In gardens water usually imitates the forms it takes in nature, and should not include regular straight or round lines. Whately prefers water to run (what he calls 'progress'), especially if it appears to continue out of sight, thus appealing to the imagination.

Whately has firm opinions about bridges, maintaining that they are inappropriate for a lake because a circuit will take you from one shore to another without requiring a span. Their use to disguise the termination of a piece of water is queried because it has been done so often, but Walpole considered he was being too rigid and that such deceptions, even if common, cannot be condemned if their purpose was to improve the landscape.[39] Whately suggested that a large bridge, such as Walton Bridge over the Thames, should not be copied in a garden because of scale: was he perhaps thinking of the small example, actually known as Walton Bridge, in the gardens at West Wycombe, Buckinghamshire? He may not have known that Walton Bridge itself was manoeuvred, by *trompe l'oeil*, to appear to be a distant part of the grounds at Oatlands.

The steep single-arch 'Chinese' bridge is disparaged for its lack of connection with the water – 'it is often seen straddling in the air' – and for its ostentation, distracting attention from the simplicity of its function. Whately's preference is for a simple, unadorned plank bridge, but he allows for a stone bridge when grandeur or elegance is called for. A stone bridge may even be in ruinous state in 'wild and romantic scenes': it is all a matter of decorum.

Whately makes much of what he terms the 'accompaniments' of a river (or lake with some length to it). He praises the remodelling of the water at Blenheim (Brown's work), which he calls a river (although the greater part is lake), pointing out the dramatic impact of the changes, including the setting of Vanbrugh's bridge in proper proportion to the water and alterations making the banks seem less precipitate (Fig. 5). A variety of woods clothes the banks, while the bridge relates axially to the Marlborough column and the palace. All the component elements of Blenheim, however far apart, 'seem to be assembled about the water', which thereby becomes the unifying and central factor as well as complementing its surroundings. 'In size, in form, and in style, it is equal to the majesty of the scene.'

Whately believes in not disclosing all the water at one view, in the interests of variety and contrast. This was a well-established principle, Pope having spoken forty years earlier of concealing the bounds.[40] He gives as an example Wotton, saying that to have a prospect of the two-mile stretch of water would make the walk alongside tedious, but the journey is broken up by 'a succession of perpetual variety'. Even the water itself changes, from lake to river, and then undergoing a drop in level. Whately's encomia on the changes in scenery include the emotional effect of late afternoon with the setting sun shooting 'its last beams on a Tuscan portico'. In his description there are a number of features which add to our knowledge of Wotton at the time, such as the colonnaded (Palladian) bridge and the location of the Chinese House imported from Stowe. His is in fact the longest contemporary account of the place.

Although a large river may have force and power in a landscape, a rill or stream may prove to be more agile and adept, especially within woodland. In such a case a succession of small waterfalls is preferable to a grand cascade. Although Whately does not mention it, the water-filled dells of Hackfall would illustrate this perfectly.

# OF ROCKS

Whately begins with a warning that rocks in themselves are austere in character and 'may surprise, but can hardly please'. They therefore need the accompaniment of water and possibly vegetation, even signs of habitation. But as rocks are not normally encountered in a garden, Whately resorts to natural landscape for his illustrations: had he explored the sublime gardens mentioned in the Introduction, however, he would have found examples just as memorable. Three of the main sites chosen are from the Peak District in Derbyshire – Middleton Dale, Matlock (Fig. 6) and Dovedale – but they provide Whately with sufficient variety to illustrate his points about how vegetation and water can affect the impact of rocks, both visually and emotionally.

Whately divides the 'character' of rocks into dignity, terror and fancy. All have a unifying wildness, though the first category is deemed to possess less of that quality because its essence is greatness of scale, placidity and composure. Greatness is also part of terror, clearly equated by Whately with the Sublime and as enunciated by Burke, since small objects cannot produce such an effect. The New Weir in Herefordshire – a chasm between two ranges of hills that rise almost perpendicularly from the furiously swirling currents of the Wye – provides testimony. Gilpin depicts the vertical rocks in Figure 7. The whole scene spells danger and fear both for the viewer and the fishermen who ride the water in fragile, unsafe boats. But Whately allows for the 'effort of art' to be admitted in the form of the sound and smoke of the forge. The final category, the fancy, or imagination, is exemplified by the course of the Dove in Dovedale, where the river constantly changes its course, movement and appearance, and where the rocks present a kaleidoscope of size and form, combined with the plantings around and in front of them (Fig. 8). All this produces a series of scenes that Whately calls highly romantic and appealing to the fancy.

Whately's taste for rocks, which was particularly appropriate in the age of the Picturesque, may have come partly from his association with Gilpin, who valued mountainous scenery above all for picturesque effect. Gilpin had undertaken only two (non-mountainous) tours by the time *Observations* came out: he was to go on the Wye tour the same year and the Lake District in 1772. So Gilpin's comments on rocks and their effect, as published much later (1782) in his account of the Wye,[41] would not have been available to Whately. They may, however, have discussed rocks together, Gilpin having been brought up in the Lake District, and it may even have been the case that Whately's thoughts inspired Gilpin and encouraged him to seek out rocks and mountains.

Rockwork had been well established in gardens for some time, in the form of grottoes and cascades, but the emphasis on natural rocks, individual and massed, *in situ* was relatively new. Whately did not have much precedent for discussing the aesthetics of rocks, though he might have read Arthur Young's published tour of the southern counties (1768), which covered rock scenes in the Wye area such as Piercefield, which he considered particularly romantic, picturesque and sublime.[42] Whately describes Piercefield himself later on in *Observations*.

# OF BUILDINGS

Whately begins by announcing that buildings in a garden, though originally for convenience and use, are now primarily what he calls 'objects' – that is, simply for decoration in the view. For this reason they are often deficient within, for outward appearance is all. Their function as objects may be to break up a bland view or create a visual focus of interest. But there should not be too many – two or three should normally be the most in a single view. If a building is for adornment only it can be of any architectural style, from native to exotic, rustic to oriental. But Whately links this with his later section on emblem versus expression (see Introduction) by positing that a building may have 'character', meaning that its presence is expressive of something, and hence the style will be limited to that which expresses the mood, feeling or emotion best. Whately uses 'Grecian' to mean classical, for instance in contrast to Gothic: he never uses 'Roman' (or 'classical').

A building may actually determine or alter the character of a scene (though not radically) and decorum should be observed; so, for example, a temple may confer dignity or a cottage a sense of rural simplicity. Trivial ornamentation, around or inside a building, is unlikely to add anything to character. In all this Whately shows himself to be keenly aware of the emotional impact a building can have. Siting is an important consideration: thus, a hermitage should be remote or hidden, while a castle should stand out on a hill (as endorsed by Gilpin).[43] Whately quotes approvingly Milton's description of a tower 'Bosom'd high in tufted trees', which became an icon of the picturesque garden – Painshill and Blaise both had one, and Repton included this device on his trade card (Fig. 9),as well as quoting the Milton tag more than once in his Red Books. Even his adversary Richard

233

Payne Knight employed the same image in *The Landscape* (1794):

> Bless'd too is he, who, 'midst his tufted trees,
> Some ruin'd castle's lofty towers sees;
> Imbosom'd high upon the mountain's brow...[44]

While allowing for garden buildings to appear in a variety of surroundings, and with a greater or lesser degree of exposure, Whately presses for harmony, and consequently mutual enhancement, of building and setting. In this he demonstrates a taste for the *fabrique* as formulated and embodied in France by that time.[45] But all buildings should contribute to the effect of the composition as a whole.

The heart of Whately's concern with the impact of buildings is his section on ruins, treated as a category of their own. These exemplify his belief in the expressive rather than the emblematic, since a ruin creates a general emotional effect more often than a narrow, specific one which requires the engagement of the mind. Ruins appeal to the feelings and to the imagination in picturing what they, and their inhabitants, were like in bygone days. Whately affirms that genuine ruins produce the strongest effect, but he admits sham examples, although they have less impact. He prefers to see at least one substantial ruin among a straggling cluster, otherwise the remains give the impression of having been small, insignificant buildings.

Ruins had a great resonance at the time, and other authors pondered their appeal. William Shenstone declared, 'A ruin, for instance, may be neither new to us, nor majestic, nor beautiful, yet afford that pleasing melancholy which proceeds from a reflexion on decayed magnificence',[46] which was echoed by Lord Kames regarding ruins producing 'a sort of melancholy pleasure',[47] thus tapping in to the deep-seated vein of melancholy that was fashionable in eight-eenth-century Britain (and indeed much earlier), as witness the popularity of the 'Graveyard Poets' such as Gray and Edward Young. This was perceived abroad as characteristically English.

Whately's chosen illustration is Tintern Abbey, which is not, of course, in a garden. He concentrates on the ruin itself and not its setting. He draws attention to ivy and other foliage on the walls and turf on the floor, which contribute significantly to the impression of age and decay, which he believes crucial, whether a ruin is real or mock. He comments, however, that the turf is so well maintained that weeds and bushes are kept away. That was not something which met with the approval of William Gilpin, who preferred his ruins to be conspicuously neglected. At the time the abbey belonged to the duke of Beaufort (of Badminton) and, in Gilpin's view, represented, with its hilly and wooded setting, 'all together a very inchanting piece of scenery'.[48] However, he disapproved of the ruin aesthetically, with its 'vulgarity' of shape, although on close inspection it satisfied him because nature was making inroads – ivy, moss, ferns. Only the 'wild, and native rudeness' of the exterior excused the neatness within,[49] though Gilpin was not as severe on the point as he was with Fountains Abbey. One of Gilpin's two sketches is reproduced as Fig. 10; he would have deplored the later tidying up of the walks around the abbey in the interests of attracting tourists, as shown in the early nineteenth-century view here (Fig. 11), although that creates the air of a garden.

# OF ART

Whately now announces a move from nature into art, meaning art in the design of a garden, and therefore into more theoretical territory. He sees art as an accessory that, in the formal garden, took full control and as a result became excessive. The cause of the problem, Whately postulates, was that the house – and subsequent axes derived from it – determined the geometry of the garden and thus imposed design on it too heavily and overtly. He extends this argument to the approach avenue, usually straight and lined by regimented trees, and says how preferable is the 'natural' approach at Caversham, near Reading, where the drive winds in sweeping curves and up and down, continually presenting new scenes until, ascending a rise, it permits the first view of the house. Then follows a long description of the beauties of the Caversham landscape.

Whately allows that some regularity may be retained in the immediate environs of the house, but firmly judges it inadmissible out in the garden. This, as we have seen, did not go down well with Latapie, nor, of course, with many other French or continental readers. But this view had long been held by English authors: as early as 1728 Batty Langley made the oft-quoted exclamation 'Nor is there any Thing more *shocking* than a *stiff regular Garden*'[50] in referring to the impossibility of symmetry producing something new or surprising. But Whately must have been jolted on to the defensive by Latapie's response, since in his letter to him he conceded that a regular layout might be appropriate for public gardens. Artefacts such as vases, statues and terms should be close to the house so as to relate to it and to the possible formality that might surround it.

Towards the end of this section, however, Whately softens and even accepts that 'Regularity in plantations is less offensive' and that regular formations can have a degree of beauty. An avenue might add dignity to a house; but such plantings should be adopted sparingly.

236

# OF PICTURESQUE BEAUTY

This section has already been considered in the Introduction under the heading 'Whately and the Picturesque'. It may be worth adding that he may well have discussed some of the issues with Gilpin, who was so preoccupied with the subject.

# OF CHARACTER

This has been partly covered in the Introduction under the heading of 'Emblem and Expression'. By 'character', Whately understands the particular qualities or nature of the garden as expressed through its component parts, whether artificial or natural. Whately believes in instant impact and emotional effect, which can be produced by plantings or by those artefacts that have general and not specific associations – ruins, most prominently. He concludes with the assertion that emotions and the imagination, once stimulated, will spread 'till we rise from familiar subjects up to the sublimest conceptions'.

# OF THE GENERAL SUBJECT

As he proceeds to deal with the divisions of a garden, Whately looks at some general considerations, determining the essence of his four categories as the elegance of a garden, the greatness of a park, the simplicity of a farm and the pleasantness of a riding. One sits or walks in the first but rides in the last; size is one determinant, a large garden constituting what would be only a small park; buildings should accordingly be situated in a garden or farm, sometimes in a park but are unnecessary in a riding. Minute beauties, or those best observed close up, are most appropriate in garden or farm.

While prospects (distant views, panoramas) are suitable for all categories, they are most so for the park or riding. Within the garden internal scenes provide adequate compensation. While a garden and a farm share much in common, in the end they do not agree stylistically, one being for decoration and pleasure and the other for husbandry and profit.

# OF A FARM

By 'farm', Whately does not, of course, mean a farm *per se* but one which has a greater or lesser degree of garden ornamentation. The *ferme ornée* had a long tradition, going back in England at least as far as the 1720s, with Stephen Switzer's advocacy of the 'Farm-like way of Gardening'. But Whately has already committed himself in the preceding general section by concluding that 'fields profusely ornamented do not retain the appearance of a farm; and an apparent attention to produce, obliterates the idea of a garden'. This sits uneasily with his opening remarks on the farm, where he declares it was long a mistake to separate the productive part of a farm from the ornamental (in the days of the formal garden).

Whately attempts to harmonise farm and garden through the idea of *simplicity*, which perhaps goes back to Pope, who spoke of treating nature 'like a modest fair, Nor over-dress, nor leave her wholly bare' – the imagery being derived from Horace's *simplex munditiis*, based on the young man who modestly, not gaudily, braided his hair.[51] Whately goes on to conflate the two uses of 'pastoral', the poetic and pasture, in examining The Leasowes at some length, although he refers the reader to Dodsley for a fuller, more detailed description. But, for once, probably in the shadow of Dodsley, he does essay a sequential description, beginning and ending in Virgil's Grove (Fig. 12). He sums it up: 'It is literally a grazing farm lying round the house; and a walk, as unaffected and as unadorned as a common field path, is conducted through the several inclosures.' While the walk may be plain, the division between the fields, which go in and out of view, are diversified; a range of trees or a broken line, hedgerows, quickset fences, copses, groves, thickets. All is 'rural and natural', with the exception of the numerous inscriptions, which Whately does not have much time for: 'in general, inscriptions please no more than once ... those beauties and those effects must be very faint, which stand in need of the assistance'. This ties in with Whately's general preference for the expressive over the intellectual and emblematic. But he recognises and accepts the division between Shenstone's evocation of a classical Arcadia (through Latin inscriptions) and a medieval past (through Gothic architecture and Spenserian references).

Having considered The Leasowes at some length, Whately then turns his attention to the *ferme ornée* as if it was a different subject. He states that numerous attempts have been made to bring 'every rural circumstance within the verge of a garden' but none so fully as at Woburn Farm (Fig. 13). Of the 150 acres, thirty-five were decorative, about seventy-five pasture and the rest arable: 'the decorations are, however, communicated to every part'. This, according to Whately's strict definition, is the perfect example of an integrated *ferme ornée*. The walk (designed originally for practical purposes) went around the pasture in a broad belt and through the arable, though on a narrower scale: 'This walk is properly garden; all within it is farm.' Not so different from The Leasowes, some might think, but the farm and the garden were much more intimately connected at Woburn. The walk, plain for the most part at The Leasowes, which aimed at simplicity, was far more adorned and varied with colourful shrubs and creepers, and, while in some places the rich borders disappear, in others they are tiered in the 'theatrical shrubbery' manner commonly encountered.[52]

Whately's conclusion is downbeat and reinforces his earlier misgivings about uniting the pleasurable with the productive. His disagreement is with the concept of the *ferme ornée* rather than with this particular place. Woburn Farm, he declares, lacks the simplicity of a farm: 'that idea is lost in a profusion of ornament; a rusticity of character cannot be preserved amidst all the elegant decorations which may be lavished on a garden'. But he approved of the decorations in themselves.

# OF A PARK

This section is central to understanding the landscape garden – the division between park and garden. It is unfortunate that Whately, after drawing such a distinction, finds it problematic to determine their separate characteristics: 'The affinity of the two subjects is so close, that it would be difficult to draw the exact line of separation between them: gardens have lately encroached very much both in extent and in style on the character of a park', he writes, with apparent reference to Brown. Garden and park share an emphasis on the natural, but intimate and smaller-scale effects are more appropriate in a garden, while spacious scenes are more suited to a park. Wildness must not overwhelm a park; if it exists, it should be no more than a part.

If the division is blurred, an intimate union of park and garden must be secured. Whately gives two examples, Painshill and Hagley. The former is a good choice of a site split evenly between garden and park, but not solely as a park (Fig. 14). It is not easy to follow Whately's division, in the absence of a plan, but Gilpin's crude sketch of the layout at Painshill in 1772 does indicate the separation of park and garden. Basically there was a crescent of pleasure ground, or ornamented garden, adjacent to the southern boundary of the River Mole which then curved up to the Gothic Tower and ran along the plateau referred to sometimes as the Elysian Plain. The only building in the park itself, according to Gilpin, was the Turkish Tent. The garden was divided from the park by 'invisible' blue netting rather than a ha-ha to keep the livestock out: the park had a wilder character, embracing the forest and the steep slope beyond the water wheel, becoming tamer as it led the visitor back to the house and the exit. Whately agrees with Uvedale Price, who praised the 'natural' effects in the wooded western part. The description brings out many of the subtleties of Painshill, such as the illusion of the lake appearing to be larger than it is.

Hagley, on the other hand, is mostly park, with the 'excellencies both of a park and of a garden' happily blended. The park is thickly wooded (Fig. 15), but diversified by wildness and the character of the various sub-areas. Whately attributes to the gravel walks that spread into all parts the unifying thread that bestows on the park the feeling of a garden. The woodland effects are described in great detail, and to the set-piece of the view up the cascades from the Palladian bridge Whately accords a theatrical character: 'a perfect opera scene'.

The reference to the 'Tinian lawn' at Hagley harks back to Admiral Anson's global voyages, published in 1748. Thomas Martyn, in *The English Connoisseur* (1766), reported that Anson had said that the Hagley lawn, with its sheep-walks and a clump at the top, reminded him of Tinian Island and that the effect was 'rural and picturesque'.[53] It could well be that Whately had picked this up from Martyn. Latapie, who had read Anson's account, expanded on the paradisal elements of Tinian Island in his footnote to Whately at this point – the pure air, the fertile pastures bordered with flowers, the scented trees, the abundant fruit, the varied and charming views of an unequal terrain. He commented that the Spanish (whose colony it was) had driven away the native inhabitants.

# OF A GARDEN

Picking up on the theme of gravel paths, Whately affirms that their presence in general is indicative of a garden. Thus, a gravel walk around a field constitutes a garden, but if it is of turf rather than gravel then it needs to be broader and more richly decorated to convey the same idea. However, gravel paths can actually injure an estate or part that is garden if used excessively. The case study is Stowe, which is, as noted earlier, by no means a typical garden, and it contains a paddock and a home park: but it is principally an *internal* garden, with views outside playing little part. Whately recognises that it was formed in 'regular' times, but claims that most evidence of formality has been obliterated. His account is a valuable record of just how little formality had survived, and in which parts, by the mid-1760s.

In Whately's long description of Stowe there are one or two identifications that stand out for their unfamiliarity to us today: thus, the Temple of Venus (Fig. 16) is called Kent's Building, even though he was responsible for several others, and the Palladian Bridge is termed 'a Pembroke bridge' in recognition of the first model of the bridge with colonnaded superstructure by the earl of Pembroke at Wilton. With re-gard to the Grecian Valley, often considered the most 'natural' part of Stowe, Whately refrains from using the word: its character is 'grandeur' and the whole valley is dominated by a feeling of awe spreading from the Temple of Concord and Victory. He may have been caught in two minds by the valley appearing to stray from his ideals of nature and simplicity, since he avoids mentioning the sculpture (described by Latapie and the guidebooks) that mingled with the trees as single figures and groups.

His conclusion is that there are many scenes remarkable for beauty or character, but there are too many buildings, as had been thought by others. However, the steady growth of wood was progressively concealing one building from another so they could be considered separately. Stowe is, to Whately, a place of magnificence and splendour, not for silence or retirement. It is the ultimate display garden in the pantheon of landscape gardens.

## OF A RIDING

This is the most problematic category for modern readers. Even at the time it was not in general usage as a component of the landscape garden and, as we have seen, it caused Latapie some difficulty. Whately says it is 'to extend the idea of a seat', and basically it comprises a horse track in the outlying parts of an estate, but a track that is decorated with the kinds of trees and shrubs that one would find in a garden. Brown's 'belts', perimeter rides through bands of wood, would illustrate the category, though Whately does not mention them. Farm buildings can be made ornamental, perhaps as a castle or abbey: an example, not found in Whately, would be the series of castellated barns and other structures scattered over the huge estate of Badminton. An important difference between garden and riding is the pace

of movement: walking and pausing in the one, riding without stopping in the other, which reduces the impact of the
scenes and renders them 'only the amusements of the way'.

Surprisingly Whately does not choose a riding as his case
study but a 'garden similar in character to a riding', as the
contents page puts it. This is Piercefield, selected for its
outward views. Whately's account is a masterly evocation
of the panoramas, the response to them and the vantage
points that show 'some of the finest scenery in Britain', a
spot that is both romantic and picturesque (Fig. 17). It is
unfortunate that, in choosing a garden, he sacrifices the essential nature of a riding, viz. that it is experienced at some
speed, on horseback or horse-drawn. The gardens at Piercefield furnish a good many walks, which Whately duly records,
but the 'romantic' scenes of wood and rock, particularly the
Wyndcliffe, are viewed at a slow pace with frequent pauses.

# OF THE SEASONS

Despite the title of this section, it is as much concerned
with times of day as with the seasons. Both contribute to
Whately's demonstration of how the same view in a garden
changes according to the light, the position of the sun and
other circumstances, and it shows him at his most sensitive
in observing the results of such changes and how one can
accommodate change by appropriate planting and by placing buildings to optimum effect, even though that effect may
sometimes be transitory.

The case study in the section is the Temple of Concord
and Victory at Stowe in late afternoon, when the sinking sun
shines on the colonnade on the south-west and casts long
shadows across the Grecian Valley. Whately's response is
both aesthetic and emotional, and exemplifies his belief in

the 'expressive' character of a garden. He has already described the temple (Fig. 18) in the section 'Of a Garden', but
neither there nor here is there any sense or explanation of
iconography. In the earlier account it is more the emotional
impact, dignified and awe-inspiring; here it is predominantly
visual, though with a definite air of calm and mellowness
after the heat of the day. Likewise, in the previous account
of Stowe, Whately, in mentioning the Temple of Venus, describes only its exterior visual impact, not the lurid (brand-
ed by some as immoral) interior decoration or its possible
interpretation.

The remainder of the section is concerned with practical
advice for designers and planters to capitalise on the changes of the seasons or times of day. All are for aesthetic effect
(such as the provision of autumn colour), though Whately
admits that winter planting, or areas designed for winter
walking, should be for convenience and shelter, even if that
involves some sacrifice of beauty.

# CONCLUSION

Whately sums up his philosophy of garden design by declaring that anything that makes natural scenes delightful
is admissible, 'whether by immediate effects, or by suggesting a pleasing train of ideas'. Those are his criteria: scenes
must be agreeable to the senses or the imagination. But the
'genius of the place' must always be the first consideration
– one cannot copy another garden or part of it. However,
knowledge of as many gardens as possible is desirable to
appreciate the range and extent of beauties that it is possible to draw upon and add to a garden.

# NOTES

## INTRODUCTION

1 See Michael Symes, 'The Web of Wotton: Cubs, Connections and Counterpoint', in *The Grenville Landscape of Wotton House, New Arcadians Journal*, 65–6 (2009), pp. 13–23.

2 Patrick Eyres, 'Victory and Empire: Wotton's Landscape in Relation to the Contemporary Iconographies of Stowe and Kew', in *The Grenville Landscape of Wotton House*, p. 126.

3 Horace Walpole's notes on the preface by William Mason to *An Heroic Epistle to Sir William Chambers, Knight* (1773), in *Satirical Poems* (published anonymously), W. Mason, ed. P. Toynbee (Oxford: Clarendon Press, 1926), p. 45. The fourteenth edition of 1777 is reproduced in this edition.

4 William Gilpin, 'A short Account of Different people with whom Mr. G. was more or less intimate in the several periods of his life', ms, quoted in C.P. Barbier, *William Gilpin: His Drawings, Teaching, and Theory of the Picturesque* (Oxford: Clarendon Press, 1963), p. 38 n 4.

5 *Ibid.*

6 *Ibid.*

7 *Ibid.*, p. 48.

8 *Ibid.* (letter from Gilpin to William Mason, 5 June 1788), pp. 120–21.

9 Thomas Whately, *Remarks on some of the characters of Shakespeare* (London: T. Payne, 1785), p. 7.

10 See especially John Dixon Hunt, *The Afterlife of Gardens* (London: Reaktion Books, 2004), pp. 137–44, and his essay, 'Emblem and Expression in the Eighteenth-Century Landscape Garden', in *Gardens and the Picturesque* (Cambridge, MA, and London: MIT, 1992), pp. 75–102.

11 Katja Grillner, 'Experience as imagined: writing the eighteenth-century landscape garden', in *Experiencing the Garden in the Eighteenth Century*, ed. Martin Calder (Bern: Peter Lang, 2006), pp. 37–64.

12 For example, Michael Leslie, 'History and Historiography in the English Landscape Garden', in *Perspectives in Garden History*, ed. Michel Conan (Washington, DC: Dumbarton Oaks, 1999) pp. 91–106 and Stephen Bending, 'Horace Walpole and Eighteenth-Century Garden History', *Journal of the Warburg and Courtauld Institutes*, 57 (1994), pp. 200–226.

13 *Observations on Modern Gardening...* (London: West and Hughes, 1801).

14 *The Works in Verse and Prose of William Shenstone, Esq.* (London: R. & J. Dodsley, 1764), Vol. 2, pp. 333–71.

15 See Michael Symes, *The Picturesque and the Later Georgian Garden* (Bristol: Redcliffe Press, 2012), p. 21.

16 Batty Langley, *New Principles of Gardening* (London, 1728), pp. 203–6.

17 Joseph Spence, *Observations, Anecdotes, and Characters of Books and Men*, ed. J.M. Osborn (Oxford: Clarendon Press, 1966), Vol. 1, p. 255.

18 Henry Home, Lord Kames, *Elements of Criticism* (Edinburgh, 1774, orig. 1762), Vol. 2, p. 432.

19 See Mavis Batey, 'The Magdalen Meadows and the Pleasures of Imagination', *Garden History*, 9:2 (1981), pp. 110–17.

20 Archibald Alison, *Essay on the Nature and Principles of Taste* (Edinburgh: Archibald Constable & Co., and London: Longman, Hurst, Rees, Ormond and Brown, 1815), 4th edn, Vol. I, p. 23.

21 *Ibid.*, p. 48.

22 *Ibid.*, p. 27.

23 *Ibid.*, p. 54.

24 *Ibid.*, pp. 58–9.

25 Horace Walpole, *The History of the Modern Taste in Gardening* [1770] (New York: Ursus Press, 1995), p. 55.

26 *Monthly Review*, 44 (1771), p. 354.

27 Humphry Repton, *Observations on the Theory and Practice of Landscape Gardening* (London: J. Taylor, 1803), p. 60.

28 George Mason, *An Essay on Design in Gardening* (London: B. & J. White, 1795), pp. 149 ff.

29 *Ibid.*, p. 151.

30 *Ibid.*

31 *Ibid.*, p. 155.

32 *Ibid.*, p. 157.

33 *Ibid.*, p. 161.

34 Quoted in *The Genius of the Place: The English Landscape Garden 1620–1820*, ed. John Dixon Hunt and Peter Willis (London: Elek Books, 1975), p. 335.

# COMMENTARY

35  William Marshall, *On Planting and Rural Ornament* (London: G. & W. Nicol, G. & J. Robinson, T. Cadell and W. Davies, 1803) (orig. 1785), 3rd edn, Vol. 1, p. 251.

36  Walpole, *History*, pp. 52–3.

37  *Shenstone's Works*, Vol. 2, p. 125.

38  Count Frederick Kielmansegge, *Diary of a Journey to England in the Years 1761–1762*, trans. Countess Kielmansegg (London: Longmans & Co., 1902), pp. 55–6.

39  Walpole, *History*, p. 55.

40  Alexander Pope, 'Epistle to Lord Burlington' [1731], *Alexander Pope's Collected Poems*, ed. Bonamy Dobrée (London: Dent, 1956), p. 248, l. 56.

41  William Gilpin, *Observations on the River Wye* [1770](London: R. Blamire, 1783), 2nd edn, pp. 23–5.

42  Arthur Young, *A Six Weeks Tour through the Southern Counties of England and Wales* (London: W. Nicoll, 1768), pp. 130–44.

43  Gilpin, *River Wye*, p. 46.

44  Richard Payne Knight, *The Landscape* (London: W. Bulmer and co., 1794), Book Two, p. 36, ll. 258–60.

45  See Michael Symes, 'The Concept of the *Fabrique*', *Garden History*, 42:1 (2014), pp. 120–27.

46  *Shenstone's Works*, Vol. 2, p. 126.

47  Lord Kames (Henry Home), *Elements of Criticism* [1762] (Edinburgh, 1774), 5th edn, p. 437.

48  Gilpin, *River Wye*, p. 46.

49  *Ibid.*, p. 50.

50  Batty Langley, *New Principles of Gardening* (London, 1728), Introduction, p. xi.

51  See Mavis Batey, *Alexander Pope: The Poet and the Landscape* (London: Barn Elms, 1999), p. 32.

52  See Mark Laird, *The Flowering of the Landscape Garden: English Pleasure Grounds 1720–1800* (Philadelphia: University of Pennsylvania Press, 1999), pp. 102–9: Joseph Spence drew a sketch of the 'tiering', p. 103.

53  (Thomas Martyn), *The English Connoisseur* (London: L. Davis and C. Reymers, 1766), Vol. 1, p. 67.

# FURTHER READING

## EIGHTEENTH-CENTURY TEXTS

Burke, Edmund, *A Philosophical Enquiry into the Origin of our Ideas of the Sublime and Beautiful*, London, 1757, amplified 1759

Chambers, William, *A Dissertation on Oriental Gardening*, London, 1772

Dalrymple, John, *An Essay on Landscape Gardening* (c1760), London, 1823

Gilpin, William, *Observations on the River Wye, and several parts of South Wales, &c...*, London, 1782

Knight, Richard Payne, *The Landscape*, London, 1794, annotated 1795

Marshall, William, *Planting and Ornamental Gardening: A Practical Treatise*, London, 1785

Mason, George, *An Essay on Design in Gardening* (rev. edn), London, 1795

(Mason, William), *An Heroic Epistle to Sir William Chambers, Knight*, London, 1773

Mason, William, *The English Garden: A Poem* (four vols), London, 1771(2)–81

Price, Uvedale, *An Essay on the Picturesque*, London, 1794

Repton, Humphry, *Sketches and Hints on Landscape Gardening*, London, 1795

Shenstone, William, 'Unconnected Thoughts on Gardening', *The Works in Verse and Prose of William Shenstone, Esq.*, Vol. 2, London, 1764

Trusler, John, *Elements of Modern Gardening*, London, 1784

Walpole, Horace, *The History of the Modern Taste in Gardening* (1770), republished New York, 1995

# MODERN SURVEYS OF THE LANDSCAPE GARDEN

Bending, Stephen (ed.), *A Cultural History of Gardens, Vol. 4: In the Age of Enlightenment*, London, 2013

Chambers, Douglas D.C., *The Planters of the English Landscape Garden: Botany, Trees, and the Georgics*, New Haven, 1993

Clark, H.F., *The English Landscape Garden*, London, 1948, reissued Stroud, 1980

Coffin, David, *The English Garden: Meditation and Memorial*, Princeton, 1994

Eyres, Patrick (ed.), *New Arcadian Journal*, various issues, mostly on political aspects of eighteenth-century gardens

Hunt, John Dixon and Willis, Peter (eds), *The Genius of the Place: The English Landscape Garden 1620–1820*, anthology of original texts, London, 1975

Hunt, John Dixon, *The Figure in the Landscape: Poetry, Painting, and Gardening during the Eighteenth Century*, Baltimore, 1976

Hunt, John Dixon (ed.), *Journal of Garden History* 13: 1 & 2, 1993 – essays on the landscape garden

Hussey, Christopher, *English Gardens and Landscapes 1700–1750*, London, 1967

Jacques, David, *Georgian Gardens: The Reign of Nature*, London, 1983

Laird, Mark, *The Flowering of the Landscape Garden: English Pleasure Grounds 1720–1800*, Philadelphia, 1999

Laird, Mark, *A Natural History of English Gardening 1650–1800*, New Haven, 2015

Malins, Edward, *English Landscaping and Literature 1660–1840*, London, 1966

Mowl, Timothy, *Gentlemen & Players: Gardeners of the English Landscape*, Stroud, 2000

Richardson, Tim, *The Arcadian Friends: Inventing the English Landscape Garden*, London, 2007

Symes, Michael, *The Picturesque and the Later Georgian Garden*, Bristol, 2012

Turner, Roger, *Capability Brown and the Eighteenth-Century English Landscape*, London, 1985, revised edition, Stroud, 1999

Williamson, Tom, *Polite Landscapes: Gardens and Society in Eighteenth-Century England*, Stroud, 1995

# INDEX OF PLACES

These are the places described or mentioned by Whately, and page references are in **bold** to indicate where they feature in his text and plain if they occur elsewhere.